CHILDREN AND THE MEDIA

CHILDREN AND THE MEDIA

Edited by

Everette E. Dennis
and Edward C. Pease

TRANSACTION PUBLISHERS
New Brunswick (U.S.A.) and London (U.K.)

ƧƧCCA

Library of Congress Catalog Number: 95-46958
ISBN: 1-56000-872-5
Printed in the United States of America

Library of Congress Cataloging-in-Publication Data

Children and the media / edited by Everette E. Dennis and Edward C. Pease.
   p. cm.
Originally published in the Fall 1994 issue of Media studies journal.
Includes bibliographical references and index.
ISBN 1-56000-872-5
1. Mass media and children. I. Dennis, Everette E. II. Pease, Edward C.
P94.5.C55C47   1996
302.23'083—dc20   95-46958
                                                            CIP

Contents

Preface   xiii

Introduction   xvii

Part I Overview

1. Symposium I   3
    Jana Eisenberg

In the first of four "symposia" of short observations on the intersection
of children and media compiled by New York free-lancer Jana Eisenberg,
six preeminent commentators share their thoughts: U.S. Secretary of
Education Richard W. Riley, Vivian Horner of Bell Atlantic, Ernest Boyer
of the Carnegie Foundation, Sen. Paul Simon of Illinois and entertainers Shari Lewis and Art Linkletter.

2. The Moment of Truth   9
    Reed Hundt

Who better to reflect on the future of children and the media than the
chairman of the Federal Communications Commission? "Why focus on
connecting our children to the potential of the communications revolution?" he asks in outlining his goals in this area. "Because any concept
of a well-ordered society depends on raising our children to participate
in public discourse, and that discourse will increasingly be through electronic means."

3. "As I Told the FCC..."   13
    Yet Another Modest Proposal for Children's Television
    Peggy Charren

After a quarter-century, the founder of Action for Children's Television
is anything but shy about telling the FCC what's wrong with commercial broadcasting for children. "The record of those 25 years shows that
in large part, commercial television has abdicated its educational responsibility and concentrated on its ability to amuse," she says. "Part of
the reason we keep having this discussion is that the commercial TV
industry does not know how—or does not care—to obey the law."

4. Why Kids Hate Educational TV   21
    Patricia Aufderheide

"You don't have to get up early too many Saturday mornings with the kids before you're convinced that there's not much educational and informational programming for children on commercial broadcast television," observes a media researcher and communication professor at the American University in Washington. "And, by and large, what is there isn't very inspiring. What was Newton Minow's line? The Vast Wasteland is perhaps vastest on Saturday mornings."

5. Electronic Childhood   29
    Ellen Wartella

"My children are living an electronic childhood," writes the dean of the College of Communication at the University of Texas-Austin. "As parents, teachers and television producers observe our children in this electronic world, we are both awed by their agility with media that sometimes intimidate us and fearful of the ways those new media are changing the nature of children's lives and the society in which they grow up."

Part II Covering Children

6. Symposium II   41
    Jana Eisenberg

Opening this section are reflections from six more commentators with vast experience writing, researching, entertaining and thinking about kids: author and journalist Alex Kotlowitz, Harvard scholar Gerald Lesser, Linda Ellerbee of "Nick News," kidpaper publisher Adam Linter, children's entertainer Raffi and Columbia University's Samuel Freedman.

7. From Unseen and Unheard to Kidsbeat   47
    Cathy Trost

"For years, the children's beat was the Rodney Dangerfield of American newsrooms," reflects the director of the Casey Journalism Center for Children and Families at the University of Maryland, "it got no respect." "Covering politics or City Hall was the journalist's dream job, and few wanted to get sidetracked into the low-status, soft-news backwater of kids." But that's changing.

8. How the News Media "See" Kids   57
   Dale Kunkel

The author, a University of California-Santa Barbara communication professor, reports on his study of how kids are covered by major U.S. newspapers and the network news. The result: a picture of coverage that is uneven and spotty at best. "By serving as gatekeepers of the messages the public receives about the condition of children in American society," he points out, "the press plays a pivotal role in influencing awareness of child-related issues."

9. Children Like Me—Where Do We Fit In?   63
   María Elena Gutiérrez

The author, a child development expert in the Alameda, Calif., elementary schools, worries about how the kids she works with in an increasingly ethnically diverse school system pattern their behavior toward one another. "American television's perception of what is beautiful, desirable, 'cool' is not where the U.S. population is heading," she argues. "But we and our children still learn from the images television projects, lessons that conform less and less to the world around us."

Part III The Child Audience

10. Symposium III   69
    Jana Eisenberg

Setting the scene for this section are five more experts with wide experience in kid audiences—Fred Rogers of "Mr. Rogers' Neighborhood," University of California-Berkeley sociologist and media scholar Todd Gitlin, Rep. Patricia Schroeder of Colorado, Craig Neff, managing editor of *Sports Illustrated for Kids,* and mass communication scholar Jane D. Brown of the University of North Carolina-Chapel Hill.

11. By the Numbers—What Kids Watch   73
    Larry McGill

"Amidst all the concern about children's exposure to potentially harmful TV, surprisingly little attention has been paid to what kids actually watch," writes The Freedom Forum Media Studies Center's director for research and administration in reporting on his own study of child viewing patterns. "While kids do flock to cartoons, PBS and Nickelodeon, data suggest these sources represent less than half of what kids spend their time watching."

12. Six Myths About Television and Children 77
     Milton Chen

"A curious mythology has grown up around television and its effects on children," observes the director of the Center for Education and Lifelong Learning at KQED in San Francisco, as he sets about debunking those myths. "Together, they would have us believe that TV is single-handedly turning kids into couch potatoes, frying their brains, shortening their attention spans and lowering their academic abilities." This is much too simplistic of you, he argues.

13. "Ask Beth" 85
     Elizabeth C. Winship

"Kids used to write me about acne, bras, long hair (boys'), short hair (girls'), nylons, tube tops, 'Mom makes me come home at 9:30!' and 'Should I kiss a boy on the first date?'" reminisces the author of a syndicated column since 1963. Times have changed for kids and how they use her newspaper-mediated advice. "Now they write me about venereal warts and condoms and suicide and drug addiction."

14. "Sesame Street" and Children in Poverty 93
     Keith W. Mielke

Since the late 1960s, Big Bird, Bert and Ernie, Oscar the Grouch and the rest of the residents of "Sesame Street" have been using TV to teach kids—especially those who need it most, observes the author, senior researcher at the Children's Television Workshop. "'Sesame Street' is reaching and helping low-income children who have a narrower range of educational opportunities in the critical preschool years—important elements in a national strategy for reaching our educational goals for the year 2000," he suggests.

15. Teaching Media Literacy—Yo! Are You Hip to This? 103
     Renée Hobbs

"Media literacy is not a new subject area, and it is not just about television—it is literacy for the information age," writes the director of the Harvard Institute on Media Education, a media-literacy program. "Media literacy advocates often refuse to line up with those who have a more traditional perspective on children's TV, who intone the merits of public broadcasting and the evils of popular, mass audience fare, championing 'good' shows and decrying the 'bad.' It may not be so important what you watch, but how you watch it."

16. Growing Media Smarts—The New Mexico Project   113
   Kate Moody

Travel to Las Cruces, N.M., and you'll find the first statewide media literacy project in the country. The author, a children's media expert from Hunter College in New York, made that trip. "One seed for growing a more media-literate, adaptable, employable, responsible and knowledgeable citizenry has started to sprout in the sands of New Mexico," she reports. "Here schools are preparing tomorrow's citizens for life in a nation where they'll receive most of their news and entertainment from television."

Part IV   Kids Making Media

17. Symposium IV   121
   Jana Eisenberg

This final roundtable session of journalists, scholars and media owners discusses the ultimate question concerning kids and the media—how to help them make their own. We convene two 13-year-old magazine writers from Duluth, Minn., Erin and Julia Hart; *Newsday*'s special projects editor Bill Zimmerman; Yale child psychologist Edward Zigler; Christopher Dahl, president of the Minneapolis-based kids' radio network Radio AAHS; and Allen Francis, a 19-year-old journalist from Marymount Manhattan College.

18. A Voice and the Courage to Use It   125
   Robert Clampitt and Stephen Silha

"If news media really want to cover communities effectively, they will need to rethink dramatically how they cover children and children's issues," write two leaders of Children's Express, a Washington-based organization for kids' own journalism. "A powerful way for media to 'mediate' the future is to invite children to become part of the journalistic enterprise—both as vital subjects and as reporters and editors." They explain how that works and what lessons "adult journalism" can learn from it.

19. News Advisory—Listen to the Children   135
   Susan Herr and Dennis Sykes

"However worthy its intentions, the quality of most journalism that examines the lives of inner-city children is compromised because editors and reporters suffer from what we call 'paternal journalism,' the notion that media can provide readers with 'detailed knowledge' about people's lives without including the voices of those people," argue the authors, directors for Youth Communication, a Chicago kids and media organization. Their solution? Let young people speak for themselves.

20. Our Own Voices, Please   141
    Marjani Coffey

The author, a 16-year-old Chicago high school junior and a reporter for *New Expression,* a monthly newspaper written for and by teens, offers a view of "paternal journalism" from the receiving end. "An auto mechanic wouldn't be asked to report on nuclear physics," she writes. "Why should an adult report on teens without experience on being a teen in the 1990s?"

21. Harlem Snapshot—Schooling in New Technologies   143
    Josiah Brown

On 123rd Street in Harlem, an innovative program at PS 125 is demonstrating the power and potential the promised new technologies can have on the lives of kids everywhere. At the Ralph Bunche School for Science and Technology, computers and interactivity are attracting growing numbers of young people, as the author, a former Freedom Forum Media Studies Center staff member, reports: "What the students experience are not just the wonders of technology, but also the consequences if their benefits are not widely available."

22. Coming Up Next...A Brighter Tomorrow for Kids' TV   151
    Karen W. Jaffe

"Even though the riches embedded in children's TV have driven some programmers to new lows," observes the executive director of KIDSNET, "there are bright spots to report." The FCC still has not enacted regulations to enforce the Children's Television Act of 1990, she points out, although she remains optimistic that technology and bureaucracy—together—will combine to revolutionize kids' television.

Part V Books and Organizations

23. Smarter Than We Think—Kids, Passivity and the Media   161
    Katharine E. Heintz

"The relationship between children and electronic media worries parents, educators and the general public," observes a University of Washington communication professor in her critical review of six key books in the field of children and media. "But this comes as no surprise, since historically every new medium has been followed by widespread concern about its potential effects on children."

24. The Guardians of Growing Up—   175
    A User's Guide to Children and Media Research Groups
    Dirk Smillie

"The landscape of groups devoted to children and the media is filled with far more than advocates and activists," reports The Freedom Forum Media Studies Center's descriptive survey of selected institutes and study centers grappling with issues affecting kids in the information age.

For Further Reading   185

Index   191

Preface

Public discussion of the media in the United States is usually framed by the assumption that the media are largely private enterprises and therefore not often subject to government intervention. The First Amendment was the framers' shield against government interference with the media. There is, however, at least one major exception to this "hands off" policy, and it involves children.

Whether it is violence on television or in the movies, newspaper publication of the names of juveniles or pornography on the Internet, the protection of children is often a rationale for public and political involvement with the media in a country where there has been little public policy toward the system of communication, save one that followed a laissez-faire approach. Thus, the detrimental effects of movies, comic books and video games, as well as efforts to reach the child as consumer, over the last half century have made the nexus between children and media vital and important.

This volume takes issue with the long-held assumption that the media are produced by adults for adults and about adults. While that may be true in the main, it does not hold completely and has often muted the role of the child on the receiving end of media fare. The child is, in fact, a consumer of the media and increasingly children are producers of media products and content—both indirectly in market studies and directly as enterprising creators of new media for children.

Increasingly, too, children are the subject of media content as they are written about, probed and scrutinized. Some of the fare about children in the media—print and broadcast, as well as new electronic services—is also directed toward children. Until recently, there has been precious little conscious attention to news coverage of and about children, but now that is changing.

Children and the Media, as developed and played out in this book is, about the complex relationship of policies involving media access and use by children historically and in the present, as well as the coverage of children in news media. And as indicated earlier, it also takes up "kids making media."

For me, this project began twenty years ago in a study of media coverage of children and childhood. That took me into an exploration of the history of childhood and the history of media's involvement with children. With a coauthor, I discovered that the "media behavior" of children was indeed worthy of attention since children were both the fodder for media content and actually consumers of media themselves. And studies I encountered also provided systematic evidence for what parents have known all along—that children learn about politics and consumption through the media and, in turn, have some considerable influence on their families in this regard.

The impetus for this book produced at The Freedom Forum Media Studies Center at Columbia University was, in part, projects by fellows at the Center studying children and media, notably Gerald Lesser of Harvard and Ellen Wartella of the Universities of Illinois and Texas, both students of children and television. In the process of scoping out prospects for this book, we benefited from the able assistance of Iris Chen, a fellow of the Coro Foundation, who did an internship at the Center. Next, a rigorous roundtable discussion helped us identify "must topics" and "essential authors." Taking part in that were television critic and author Les Brown; Peggy Charren, the spirited founder of Action for Children's Television; Robert Clampett, who created "Children's Express"; sociologist Steven Gorelick of the Graduate School of the City University of New York; author and journalist Don Guttenplan; Karen Jaffe of KIDSNET; Cathy Trost, who heads the Casey Journalism Center for Children and Families at the University of Maryland; Rosemarie Truglio, an expert on children and media at Columbia's Teacher's College in New York; journalist Joanne Wasserman of the *New York Daily News,* who actually covers children for the mass audience, and Judy Wessler of the Children's Defense Fund New York Child Health Project. To these generous and creative thinkers, we are grateful.

I am indebted to co-editor Ted Pease for his efforts in operationalizing and editing the *Media Studies Journal* volume on which this book is based. Also deserving commendation are the *Journal*'s associate editor, Lisa DeLisle, and editorial assistants Nathaniel Daw and Jennifer Kelly. As always, my superb assistant Cate Dolan played a key role in working with many parties involved in this book.

As always, this volume and others we have done with Transaction Publishers owes inspiration and support to Irving Louis Horowitz, who believed this was a worthwhile venture and greatly encouraged our efforts.

Everette E. Dennis
Senior Vice President,
The Freedom Forum
Arlington, Va.
December 1995

Introduction

*"And shall we just carelessly allow children to hear
any casual tales which may be devised by casual
persons, and to receive in their minds for the most
part the very opposite of those which we should
wish them to have when they're grown up?"*

—Plato
The Republic

*"A child should always say what's true
And speak when he is spoken to...."*

—Robert Louis Stevenson
The Whole Duty of Children

In large part, the mass media are produced by adults, for adults, about
adults. That's true of virtually all forms of media, print and electronic,
from books to on-line databases. The very mention of children and the
media conjures up a marginal image somewhere out on the periphery of
the media world of grown-ups. There are and always have been exceptions, of course, ranging from children's books and magazines to newspaper supplements and children's television, not to mention recorded
music, video games and other new media applications. Still, these media have always stayed on a limited reservation, playing a secondary
role in institutions and industries largely run by, concerned with and
aimed at adults.

Now that is changing and changing dramatically as the new frontier
of media for, about, and increasingly *by* children is making a dramatic
imprint on communication. While the impact of media on children—
especially content that contains violence and sex—is frequently in the
news as the topic of public debate, the children's media scene is far
broader and deeper than that. Beyond the impact of TV on children,
there is widespread interest in children as an audience that is clearly
connected to more media content for kids. At the same time, media enterprises created by children, sometimes with the help of adults, are a

growth industry. All this intuitive discovery has media industries at long last catching up with research. As the editor-in-chief of the *Media Studies Journal* wrote in a 1976 article in *Journalism Quarterly:*

> If anything, communication research on children's media behavior suggests that children are indeed attentive to public affairs coverage and are thereby worthy of courting as an audience. Consumer behavior studies also point up the role of children in parental buying decisions, and political socialization studies indicate the importance of media in determining attitudes of future voters.

While newspapers have long treated children's activities and problems as a source of news, they have also courted children as an audience since at least the 19th century through treatment of children's parties, games and other endeavors, as well as the more horrific depiction of the suffering of children in the years after the Industrial Revolution in urban factories and slums. Images of children have long been part of the iconography of war. Within the last year, for example, ABC News featured interviews with children in war-torn Bosnia, while the *New York Times* explained how children's crayon drawings tell of Rwanda's horror.

Political coverage, too, has tuned in on children in dramatic ways in recent times. The race for governor of Texas in 1994 had both candidates framing top issues around kids, which moved Kay Hollestelle of the Children's Foundation to assert that "the bottom line is that children make good issues, but they don't vote."

Or do they? Documentarian Linda Ferris in a recent report on kids and the media tested the proposition that "Children are frequently portrayed in the media: on TV, in newspapers, in commercials, on billboards, in fairy tales and cartoons. But as a general rule they are objects, rather than subjects of communication. They rarely use the media themselves, or determine the contents of messages." In her study of "Children Making Television in Guatemala," Ferris had reason to challenge some of those assumptions, as have others in recent years who are part of a new trend that takes kids seriously, both as *objects* and *subjects* of communication and as audience members and communicators, although not yet on a level with grown-ups.

Kids may not "vote" in the conventional political sense, but they do consume media, inspire the creativity of advertisers and others who want to have a hearing with children who will, they reason, in turn influence their parents, either with friendly persuasion or tantrums. The media industries are aware of all this and are clearly targeting children as consumers of media ranging from movies and videos to advertisements on cereal boxes.

Conferences, seminars and various university, foundation and industry reports have been alive with suggestions for greater and more extensive coverage of children in the media as well as closer looks at child viewers and readers, media literacy and related topics. Indeed several centers for the study of media and children have developed while others are on the drawing boards, and at least one leading editor has declared that the "kids' beat is the hottest thing going today to build circulation and improve literacy."

Children, the portion of the human community residing between birth and puberty, in 1995 will constitute 22 percent of the U.S. population and 32 percent of the world's humanity. While much attention has been given to the graying of America and other countries, far less focuses on the burgeoning child population in many developing countries as well as in the United States.

While the material that follows is largely concerned with the American media scene as it pertains to children, the global community is replete with old and new media for and about children. In addition, some exemplary U.S. productions, such as "Sesame Street," are exported abroad to considerable success.

Some commentators, notably the French historian Phillipe Aries, argue that childhood as a state of mind and identity zone is an "invention" of the modern world, giving rise to considerable discussion of changing adult perceptions of the child and how children themselves experience childhood. Though disputed by some, the notion that children were once viewed as "little adults" pervades the history of art and that of work as well. While children are mentioned in the Bible and in the writings of Plato, the idea that they ought to be protected, catered to and nurtured is a fairly recent notion in public discourse. That they are a constituency for the media in all of its functions—news and information, opinion, entertainment and marketing—is itself rather revolutionary.

It is this realization, and the debate over its appropriateness, that infuses the connections between media and children, making them a matter of high priority in the modern media society. From debates in Congress about the detrimental effects of movies, comic books and video games over the last century to efforts to court children as media consumers, there is a clear recognition that the media are not now and probably never were *purely* adult fare *per se*. Children have been looking over the shoulders of their parents since the beginning of civilization and continue to do so today, even in an era of media for, by and about children.

With this book, it is our desire to go beyond predictable debates over children and media by moving through the various avenues, from consumer to producer, with the hope that this will both stimulate more disciplined intelligence on the topic and lead to continuing creative efforts to engage a sometimes neglected part of the human community.

In *Children and the Media*, we recognize the far-reaching importance of the media-child connection with an effort to "map" the territory at the verge of a widening electronic world. In this cartographic enterprise, we divide the topic into four areas—an overview of the issues; a look at what some editors have called the "next great beat"—kidsbeats; children as media consumers; and, finally, a report on kids who make their own media. In this endeavor, we have convened 23 authors who study and practice in the world of kids' media. We also contacted dozens of performers, producers, researchers and scholars for their short takes on what issues regarding kids and media deserve the most attention; the insights of 23 of these commentators appear in four "symposia" that lead each section of *Children and the Media*.

Leading this volume is "Overview—Children and the Media," beginning with the first of four "symposia" compiled by New York writer Jana Eisenberg. These opening insights on some of the broad issues affecting children and the media in the 1990s come from six commentators who know whereof they speak. In Symposium I, "Before the Show Starts," U.S. Secretary of Education Richard W. Riley, Vivian Horner of Bell Atlantic Video Services, Ernest Boyer of the Carnegie Foundation, Sen. Paul Simon, D-Ill., entertainer Shari Lewis (with Lamb Chop's counsel) and kidshow legend Art Linkletter outline some of the issues that propel and trouble events when kids and media intersect.

These short takes serve as a broad backdrop for four scene-setting essays that outline some of the issues concerning media, kids, entertainment, kids, merchandising, kids and regulatory concerns. Who better to outline the debate than Reed Hundt, chairman of the Federal Communications Commission? In his remarks, "The Moment of Truth," Chairman Hundt explains how he sees new telecommunications technologies as a savior of modern education.

Next, with a critic's eye, comes Peggy Charren, who founded Action for Children's Television a quarter-century ago because she was so outraged by what television did and didn't provide children. In this account of "As I Told the FCC...," Charren outlines "yet another modest proposal" to unburden commercial television of a task she says it neither wants nor can perform. Instead of having to mess with quality children's programming, she says, the networks should simply be assessed a tax on their revenues, payable to the Public Broadcasting Service, which does know how to do the job. Then both commercial and public broadcasting could concentrate on what they do best.

Many credit Charren with forcing passage of the federal Children's Television Act of 1990, which was heralded as ushering in a new era of responsible broadcasting and cable production for America's kids. But, as Patricia Aufderheide of the American University suggests in "Why Kids Hate Educational TV," even after the 1990 Act, "the Vast Wasteland is perhaps vastest on Saturday mornings." A study by Aufderheide with the Center for Media Education in Washington confirms the sharks of children's programming are closing in again. Rounding out this section, children's media scholar Ellen Wartella, dean of the College of Communication at the University of Texas-Austin, describes in an account of her own sons' "Electronic Childhood" how mediated America appears from the trenches of parenthood.

The second section of the book looks at how the media are "Covering Children." Six expert witnesses open up in a "symposium" conversation—author and journalist Alex Kotlowitz; scholar Gerald Lesser of Harvard and the Children's Television Workshop; Linda Ellerbee, president of Lucky Duck Productions and host of Nickelodeon's "Nick News"; Adam Linter of *Tomorrow's Morning* kids' newspaper; singer/songwriter, children's entertainer and activist Raffi; and Samuel Freedman of the Columbia University Graduate School of Journalism's Fellowship Program for Children and the News.

Cathy Trost, head of the Casey Journalism Center for Children and Families at the University of Maryland, then reviews the evolution of children's news coverage in "From Unseen and Unheard to Kidsbeat." Mass communication researcher Dale Kunkel reports from the University of California-Santa Barbara on his study of "How the News Media 'See' Kids," and public school administrator María Elena Gutiérrez closes the section with a look at "Children Like Me—Where Do We Fit In?"

Opening the third section—"The Child Audience"—another panel of five experts is convened: PBS's Fred Rogers, Berkeley sociologist and media critic Todd Gitlin, Rep. Patricia Schroeder, D-Colo., Craig Neff, managing editor of *Sports Illustrated for Kids,* and media scholar Jane D. Brown of the University of North Carolina-Chapel Hill. They take part in a third "symposium" to consider how child audiences are served, exploited, manipulated and nurtured.

Their insights set the tone for pieces by six authors, beginning with The Freedom Forum Media Studies Center's director of research and administration, Larry McGill, who uses audience data to describe exactly, by the numbers, "What Kids Watch." Then Milton Chen, director of the Center for Education and Lifelong Learning at KQED in San Francisco, discusses "Six Myths About Television and Children." And Elizabeth Winship, whose syndicated newspaper column has reassured kids for 21 years, describes in "Ask Beth" how teens' worries have changed over time. Keith Mielke, senior researcher at the Children's Television Workshop, looks at how "Sesame Street" has changed the lives of children in poverty over a quarter-century. This section ends with two close-ups on media literacy efforts: Renée Hobbs, of Babson College in Massachusetts and head of Harvard's Institute on Media Education, describes the impact of "Teaching Media Literacy—Yo! Are You Hip to This?" And Kate Moody travels from New York's Hunter College to witness an innovative statewide media literacy effort in "Growing Media Smarts—The New Mexico Project."

The fourth section, "Kids Making Media," opens with the last six of our "symposium" consultants to tackle the question of "voice" and representation: Erin and Julia Hart, 13-year-old magazine writers from Duluth, Minn.; Bill Zimmerman, who manages *Newsday*'s kids' coverage; Edward Zigler, a Yale psychologist; Christopher Dahl, president of a Minneapolis-based kids' radio network; and Allen Francis, a 19-year-old New York City journalist and student. Their perspectives set the tone for four essays that throw light on the question of kids as media producers, not just consumers. Then in "A Voice and the Courage to Use It," Children's Express' Robert Clampitt and Stephen Silha describe the liberating effects of kid-built news on kids and adults alike. From Chicago, Youth Communication's Susan Herr, in her essay with Dennis Sykes, "News Advisory—Listen to the Children," adds a sharper tone in her critique of what the "mainstream" adult press establishment finds praiseworthy. They are accompanied by Marjani Coffey, a 16-year-old junior at St. Ignatius College Prep in Chicago and a member of the staff of Youth Communication's teen newspaper, *New Expression,* who asks for "Our Own Voices, Please." Those voices are starting to be heard (and seen), as The Freedom Forum Media Studies Center's Josiah Brown describes in his trip to Manhattan's PS 125 in "Harlem Snapshot—Schooling in New Technologies." And, finally, Karen Jaffe, who directs Washington's KIDSNET, predicts improvements in the children's media arena in "Coming Up Next...A Brighter Tomorrow for Kids' TV."

Katharine Heintz of the University of Washington puts the ribbon on this package of hopes, dreams, fears, research, measurement, speculation and insight on how media and kids interact in *Children and the Media's* book review essay entitled "Smarter Than We Think—Kids, Passivity and the Media," which sums up the collected wisdom of six leading works on media and children. *Children and the Media* then offers The Freedom Forum Media Studies Center's own selective overview of programs and organizations that examine the intersection of kids and media in "The Guardians of Growing Up—A User's Guide to Children and Media Research Groups."

Anyone who has a kid, or who knows one, or who has been one, understands the powerful attraction the mass media hold over them. Older generations remember the power of radio, when, as children, they gathered like "The Waltons" around the living room set, or—later—toted transistorized rock 'n' roll or a baseball game to the backyard or beach. Car radio AM-FM was an essential part of growing up in the 1950s, '60s and '70s; then self-programmed cassette tapes and CDs joined the mix. On television, Shari Lewis and Lamb Chop, Captain Kangaroo and Mr. Moose, Bozo, "Romper Room" and many others shared parenting and teaching chores. Beginning in the 1970s, toddlers and parents alike welcomed Bert and Ernie, Oscar, Grover, Big Bird and all the "Sesame Street" gang into their homes—they were part of the family. In 1994, Barney the purple dinosaur may have more name recognition among the under-5 set than Big Bird, Rocky and Bullwinkle, Bill Clinton, Bozo, Sky King, Beethoven, Dick and Jane, Fred Flintstone, My Little Pony, Ringo Starr, Popeye and Horace Greeley—perhaps combined. If so, there is reason to worry that slick marketing has taken over American mass media for kids.

But some of the authors in this volume point beyond the TV-bound latchkey kids and the undersized American couch potatoes to models that don't just soak up media but use it, both in their personal lives and as a means to grow, learn and make their own voices heard.

I
Overview

1

Symposium I

Jana Eisenberg

Issues raised in scrutinizing the interaction between children and the mass media in the 1990s are so far-reaching—touching homes, schools, government, society and culture, both here and abroad, indeed, our very future—that the editors of *Children and the Media* decided to spread a somewhat wider net than usual in soliciting the thoughts of people who influence both policy and practice in this crucial arena. Author Jana Eisenberg contacted dozens of social and political leaders, media professionals, scholars, researchers and kids themselves for their sense of the core issues and concerns surrounding media and young people in this latest epoch of the brave new media world. A representative selection of these responses, in short takes, appears in each of the four sections of *Children and the Media*.

Contributors to the four "symposium" roundtables include a U.S. Cabinet secretary, two 13-year-old sister writers from Duluth, Minn., a congresswoman from Colorado, Mr. Rogers, distinguished scholars and researchers, a 19-year-old New Yorker, a U.S. senator from Illinois, legendary entertainers and authors, journalists, educators and many others. They had much to say when we asked them for their thoughts on the most crucial issues facing the coverage of children, media content for a child audience, and the question of kids' own participation in the media process.

Many of the concerns raised by our final 23 sources are familiar ones—enduring problems of violence, commercialization, trivialization and

3

the "abdication" of social and family responsibility to the "electronic babysitter." But other perhaps less obvious topics also are broached by this panel of experts—questions of young people's own unfiltered voices in the mass media, their frustration with how the media represent them, and issues of society's interest in a media literacy in the burgeoning information age.

In this first of four "symposium" discussions, "Before the Show Starts," six of our expert sources help define the issues explored in the rest of this book.

Secretary Richard W. Riley, U.S. Department of Education:

It's no secret that the print and broadcast media have a dramatic impact on children's ability to learn and their interest in learning. Yet the media have a mixed record when it comes to using their power to promote the social, emotional and intellectual growth of children.

Above all else, it is essential that children read. Reading is the starting point of learning, and reading with young children is both educationally valuable and great fun for the adults who care for them. There are many examples of creative and stimulating magazines designed for specific age groups.

In the broadcast media, while there have been wonderful successes, including high quality cable and network shows, there have also been too many blatantly commercial, inferior efforts—programming that fails to challenge young minds and engage children, and offers little positive reinforcement for learning. Children deserve the opportunity to see and hear messages that will teach, encourage and inspire.

American children watch an average of three hours of television per day, even more than a decade ago, and some watch six hours per day. Even two hours a day has been shown to have a negative impact on academic achievement. I urge American parents to limit their children to a maximum of two hours a day, even if that means that the remote control may have to disappear on occasion.

In a world with such extraordinary technological opportunities as ours, the media can and must do more to serve our children. I encourage media professionals to link education with entertainment more effectively, and to help parents and schools at every turn to challenge our young people to begin a lifetime of learning.

Vivian Horner, creator of Nickelodeon, director, children's a[...] cational services, Bell Atlantic Video Services:

My impression is that, across the board, children have gotten the short end of the stick.

Most commercial television for children is inadequate at best and damaging at worst. Broadcasters program to children only when there is no more commercially attractive audience. Children's fare is designed to engage kids' eyeballs, not their minds. Since kids generally don't have disposable incomes, TV makes them surrogate salesmen. They want something and pester their parents for it. Young children have great difficulty distinguishing between reality and fantasy, yet we advertise directly to them. While the FCC periodically sounds an alarm about the quantity and quality of children's television and its intense commercialization, interest and enforcement tend to wax and wane.

At first, cable provided more programming for kids, and mostly it didn't carry commercials. But as their audiences increased, cable networks grew to resemble broadcast networks, unable to resist the lure of advertising dollars. Almost all cable offerings for kids today are highly commercialized.

Children learn from all media. The question is *what* do they learn? Do they learn that all problems can be resolved in 28 minutes? Do they learn that disagreements are settled with fists or a gun? Do they learn what to buy? Children deserve entertainment and experiences from electronic media that result in more than "incidental" learning.

Ernest Boyer, president, Carnegie Foundation for the Advancement of Teaching:

No one can deny television's great potential. But over the past 30 years, commercial television's great promise for the education of children has faded. And while we acknowledge that "fantasy" has a rightful place in enriching children's perspective, the fantasy world of commercial television is often an irresponsible approach to entertaining them, let alone to nurturing their capacity to learn and grow.

The multibillion-dollar television industry has decreed that the airwaves are overwhelmingly for adults, not children. Edward Palmer, author of *Television and America's Children*, has said, "It is economically irresponsible that we fail to use television fully and well to help meet nationwide...educational deficiencies."

Television sparks curiosity and opens up distant worlds to children. Through its magic, youngsters can travel to the moon, the bottom of the ocean or inside a cell. They can visit medieval castles and climb mountains. They are exposed to science, technology, history and art—all with a flick of the wrist. Let's use the exciting, almost unlimited potential of the electronic teacher to uplift rather than degrade. By so doing, we will improve the quality of education and, ultimately, help secure the future of the nation.

The 1990s could be the decade when television's promise to children is finally fulfilled. What is needed is a more coherent policy established not just by government but by concerned citizens and committed leaders in the industry itself. The promise is to enrich the lives of all children, to give them an exciting new window to the world.

Newton Minow recently said, "A new generation now has the chance to put the vision back into television, to travel from the wasteland to the promised land, and to make television a saving radiance in the sky." I could not agree more.

Sen. Paul Simon, D-Ill.:

Adults and children watch too much television. In the inner cities— high crime areas—kids watch more television than they do nationally. Because we have let education deteriorate and tolerated a high level of adult illiteracy, many parents are not able to enrich their kids much. Alternatives to television are limited.

The glorification of violence has a real impact. It is a factor in the crime problem. And when the former president of the United States, George Bush, as well as kids, say, "Make my day," what they are saying is violence is fun as well as a way of solving a problem.

We are gradually—not dramatically—moving away from the glorification of violence. The phenomenon is similar to what has happened with cigarettes and alcohol. If you look at some old films, you'll see heroes and heroines smoking a great deal and drinking very heavily. That has gradually changed, and in the process we have modified the habits of the people. It's a cultural thing. And I think the same thing will happen in terms of violence.

I got interested in this subject when I turned on a television set and saw someone being sawed in half with a chainsaw, in living color. It bothered me. And I thought, "What does this do to a 10-year old?" There is an overwhelming amount of research that says that the glamorization of violence on television does harm to our society, just as cigarettes do harm to our health.

Shari Lewis, family entertainer, ventriloquist and author:

I come from a very large family, and the examples that were set provided the context for how to live. Today, the media are the storytellers and provide the examples.

Media cannot be trusted to do well when kids are available to the highest bidder, even though commercials are a fact of life—the way that things get paid for in America. All of the studies say that children who watch hostile and aggressive shows are more hostile and aggressive in the schoolyard and in the classroom. I know the network children's departments are run by very nice, intelligent, humane, family women. But they all must compete at the level of the lowest common denominator.

Another sad fact is that in spite of the many hours that children spend listening to TV and radio, their vocabularies are shrinking. Their frame of reference is broader (for example, when you were a kid, did you know where Iraq was?), but cultural references are going by the boards. Whenever I refer to "sour grapes" or "don't cry wolf," kids don't know what I am talking about. In response to that trend, I am doing a series of books based on Aesop.

America provides the media for the entire world. My daily PBS show, "Lamb Chop's Play-Along," is on the air in every English-speaking country. No matter where you go, you see American children's shows. We are influencing the conscience, behavior and standards of the entire planet. It behooves us to do a better job.

Art Linkletter, family entertainer and author:

I have always been an optimist, but now I'm becoming discouraged. In the last 20 years, children's media—except recorded music—have gotten better. But unfortunately, the worst has become worse. And there's more of it. Electronic media have replaced books. TV is used as a babysitter.

Ever since 1960, kids have listened to a stream of sex and violence in popular music. When I lectured against drug abuse, music was one of my greatest opponents: It was telling kids drugs were great.

TV and other media were not designed for education, information or even entertainment. They are billboards. My biggest complaint about TV is the state of the talk show, which I originated. The people who run these shows, particularly in the daytime, are social street sweepers, depositing mental misfits in our parlors. Children see grown-ups endorsing previously taboo behavior.

Humans have always been fascinated by sex and grotesque things. For example, when Spielberg's "ET" was released, it was also rushed into a video-game version by Atari. That product was the biggest flop in video-game history, because kids who buy those games want violence. They will go and see a sweet movie, as they do Disney's The Lion King, but when it comes to buying video games, they want smashing, burning and killing people.

I do not believe that kids, as a result of seeing make-believe violence in movies and on TV, go out and kill people. But it callouses them. So when they see the real thing on the daily news, it's just another murder.

Jana Eisenberg is a New York-based free-lance writer, formerly with New York Newsday.

2

The Moment of Truth

Reed Hundt

There is tremendous concern in this country about TV violence. The concern is justified: Violence on television is one of many causes of violence in our society, and violence is totally unacceptable in any "well-ordered society."

It should not be necessary for government to step in to deal with violence on broadcasting, but because congressional leaders such as Sens. Ernest Hollings, Daniel Inouye, Byron Dorgan and Paul Simon, and Rep. Edward Markey helped identify this issue, both the cable and television industries have announced comprehensive, industrywide anti-violence initiatives.

This fall, ABC will introduce a new on-air logo to designate certain programs as "particularly enjoyable for family viewing." Television set manufacturers have approved a standard for blocking technology that will rely on the programmers' sending their ratings electronically. A number of companies already have begun to sell devices that will enable parents to block programs.

One task we can and should assign to government, however, is to guarantee that the communications revolution reach all Americans, to ensure that we do not divide into a society of information haves and have-nots. How could we develop the consensus ethic of a well-ordered society if we were divided into groups of those who could read and write and those who could not? How could we truly compare beliefs, share aspirations, agree on facts, or reason civilly together?

Such may be the future distinction between those who have the opportunity to take advantage of modern communications and those who do not.

9

Now, some argue that by virtue of the inexorable logic of market economics, the information highway will naturally reach to all Americans who need it. Is this true? Let's look at how we are doing with regard to the oldest lane on the information highway: the wire telephone network.

In 13 states, more than one in 12 households don't have telephones. In the African American and Hispanic households representing the lowest one-quarter of income groups, 10 percent to 36 percent lack active phone service. Overall, 15 million Americans are without phones. Nearly 10 percent of children under age 6 live in homes without phones, 20 percent to 36 percent among African American and Native American children.

Is it important for these people to be connected? You bet.

And the capabilities of the humble telephone line are multiplying. The common telephone line could bring every classroom in the country—all 45 million students—onto the information highway. That line could connect the computers that are in half the classrooms in the country to a world of information. But only one out of 24 classrooms even has telephone lines.

Why focus on connecting our children to the potential of the communications revolution? Because any concept of a well-ordered society depends on raising our children to participate in public discourse, and that discourse will increasingly be through electronic means.

We can't afford to deny anyone the opportunity to enjoy the communications revolution. When we read that our children are falling behind, we are all responsible. When we learn from the Department of Education that 90 million adults—47 percent of the U.S. adult population—demonstrate low levels of literacy, we accept that as a challenge for us all.

The communications revolution could bring all these adults and all our children into the great public reasoning process that ultimately will sort out the chaos of values in this country.

I believe this from personal experience. In 1969, when all telephones were black and all dials were rotary, I spent a short time as a middle-school teacher. Only half the kids who started the seventh grade would graduate from ninth. On average, in three years at my school, a child would fall two years behind in reading skills.

The best way out—the only way out—was physically to get out. And the way to get out was to be permitted to enroll in one of the city's magnet schools, the only ticket out of an ever-deepening cycle of poverty and hopelessness.

Three students out of my 150 who started seventh grade could read well enough to qualify for a chance for admission to the magnet school. We met every Saturday for special study sessions on how to pass the entrance exam. After months, the day of the exam came.

Maybe you've seen the movie "Lean on Me," about the New Jersey principal Joe Clark, or the movie "Stand and Deliver," about East Los Angeles math teacher Jaime Escalante. Both were true stories in which the efforts of dedicated teachers vastly improved the test scores of their students. Both movies included the key to all successful movies: a happy ending.

But no movie was made about my three special students. No movies will be made. All my students failed the test. And I had failed them.

But I did make a promise to myself: I wouldn't settle for that ending. None of us should ever settle for that ending. Today's schoolchildren must have better ways to escape poverty, despair and hopelessness. We must make sure that the teachers of today are better teachers than I was, have better tools than I did, and don't bring too little too late to their mission, as I did.

The communications revolution won't guarantee happy endings for all; it is not a cure for all society's ills. But I know it presents an opportunity for our children that is far more important than simply getting more cable channels or movies on demand. The communications revolution should not be a highway—it should be a bridge between the world of opportunity and the world of despair.

I'd like to express the urgency I feel as we take on the many issues of the communications revolution. This moment in time reminds me of a hymn I used to sing in high school as part of our daily service. It said, "Once to every man and nation comes the moment to decide, in the strife of truth with falsehood, for the good or evil side."

We are now at such a moment. This is a moment to decide if we want the communications revolution to be a dawn of opportunity for everyone, for kids in all schools, for adults with low literacy levels, for those who don't even have a simple wire phone line.

This is the moment to decide whether the communications revolution will be like the tower on the plain of Shinar that brought down confoundment and scattering and division in the Sumerians. Or will it be the way to bring new understanding, tolerance and learning to all of us? Will it give us, as it can give us, the ways to build an enduring, ethical, well-ordered society?

Reed Hundt is chairman of the Federal Communications Commission. This chapter is adapted from his remarks at the Everett C. Parker Ethics in Telecommunications Luncheon in New York City on Sept. 13, 1994.

3

"As I Told the FCC..."
Yet Another Modest Proposal
for Children's Television

Peggy Charren

For 25 years—one-quarter of a century—I have begged, demanded, wheedled, argued with broadcasters and the Federal Communication Commission to get commercial television to obey the laws that are supposed to govern children's programming in this country.

The record of those 25 years shows that in large part, commercial television has abdicated its educational responsibility and concentrated on its ability to amuse. Part of the reason we keep having this discussion is that the commercial TV industry does not know how—or does not care—to obey the law. Broadcasters complain that they cannot figure it out: "What is an educational show?" If they don't know, they should be in the shoe business, not in show business. How can they fulfill their licensee obligation to serve the public if they can't tell the difference between which shows educate and which don't?

The FCC's 1974 Policy Statement is clear on this point:

> Although children's entertainment programs may have educational value (in a very broad sense of the term), we expect to see a reasonable amount of programming which is particularly designed with an educational goal in mind.... There are many imaginative and exciting ways in which the medium can be used to further a child's understanding of a wide range of areas: history, science, literature, the environment, drama, music, fine arts, human relations, other cultures and languages and basic skills such as reading and mathematics, which are crucial to a child's development.

What's to understand? Misguided or profit-mad, broadcasting is too often used to showcase not educational programs, but violence, dirty words and sexual innuendo, to the point that many adults, frustrated and angry with this fare foisted off on their children, clamor for censorship—ban G.I. Joe's guns, the Ninja Turtles' weapons and other violence, language and lyrics that anyone would agree are not suitable for young audiences.

Censorship is not the way to protect children from inappropriate television. The right to express what some may consider offensive speech is the price Americans pay for the richer freedom of political speech and expression that we cannot afford to lose. Instead, Congress passed the Children's Television Act of 1990, an effort to increase viewing options for young audiences. Under the law, commercially licensed TV stations must provide programs "specifically designed" to educate and inform children.

This is just the latest good-faith attempt by the federal government to make use of the educational and developmental potential of television. Over and over, the Congress and the FCC have singled out children's television for special consideration. Dean Burch, FCC chairman under Richard Nixon, set up the Commission's Children's Television Unit in 1971. "Broadcasters must recognize...that children are different and that the difference requires a dedicated special effort," Burch said. "The FCC should do all it can to foster the best possible governmental climate for such action."

Burch's successor, Richard Wiley, FCC chairman under Gerald Ford, vowed that the FCC would "try to bring our influence to bear for diversity in television so this great medium is used to inform as well as entertain."

Under Wiley's leadership, the 1974 Children's Television Report and Policy Statement looked like a Magna Carta for kids' TV:

> [The FCC has] consistently maintained the position that broadcasters have a responsibility to provide a wide range of different types of programs to serve their communities. Children, like adults, have a variety of different needs and interests. Most children, however, lack the experience and intellectual sophistication to enjoy or benefit from much of the non-entertainment material broadcast for the general public. We believe, therefore, that the broadcaster's public service obligation includes a responsibility to provide diversified programming designed to meet the varied needs and interests of the child audiences. In this regard, educational or informational programming for children is of particular importance....

This "importance," the Policy Statement concluded, extends far beyond the question of what children see to their participation in society. "Once these children reach the age of 18 years," the FCC said, "they are expected to participate fully in the nation's democratic process and, as one commentator [A. Meiklejohn, 1961] stated, 'Education, in all its phases, is the attempt to so inform and cultivate the mind and will of a citizen that he shall have the wisdom, the independence and, therefore, the dignity of a governing citizen.'"

Take that, Bucky O'Hare!

Rule-making on children's television continued under Charles Ferris's FCC chairmanship. In 1980, echoing Meiklejohn, Ferris said a social responsibility exists to monitor and regulate television that helps form citizen values and perspectives. "The marketplace forces of the television industry as it is presently structured fail when you apply them to children," he declared.

Which brings me back to the 1974 FCC Policy Statement, which argued that television be used "with an educational goal in mind"; as it said, "There are many imaginative and exciting ways in which the medium can be used to further a child's understanding."

I just can't understand why the nation's commercial broadcasters seem to have such trouble figuring out what kind of programming holes might "further understanding." Perhaps the United Nations declaration on the mass media at its 1989 Convention on the Rights of the Child would help: It says, in part, that mass media education should be directed to "the preparation of the child for responsible life in a free society, in the spirit of understanding, peace, tolerance, equality of sexes, and friendship among all peoples, ethnic, national and religious groups...."

Taken together with the mandate for children's programming in the 1974 FCC statement, that statement provides a meaningful prescription for the nation's media. E.B. White, who wrote some of the most enduring of children's literature, adds a further caveat worth noting: "Children are demanding," he observed. "They are the most attentive, curious, eager, observant, sensitive, quick and generally congenial readers on earth. They accept, almost without question, anything you present them with, as long as it is presented honestly, fearlessly, and clearly. Anybody who writes down to children is simply wasting his time."

But over and over, commercial broadcasters have demonstrated that educating children, that "writing up" to them, is not even on the back burner of their corporate priorities. Over and over again, America's TV industry has demonstrated that, absent close regulation, it doesn't give a damn about service to children.

During the 1960s and '70s, the FCC played a significant role in getting broadcasters to provide choices for children. But through the decade of the 1980s, all there was to hear was the drip, drip, drip of the Reagan-Bush trickle-down theory regarding communications: What was good for the industry was good for the children. "Broadcasting is a business," declared Reagan FCC Chairman Mark Fowler in September 1981. Disregard "myths about service to the community," he suggested, in favor of "reliance on the marketplace." Rely on "entrepreneurial initiatives," he advised: "Television is just a toaster with pictures."

That enlightened doctrine helped turn commercial television for young audiences into 30-minute product advertisements that make a mockery out of the legal requirement of TV stations to serve the public interest.

CBS's response to this climate was typical of the networks at the time. During the 1970s, CBS—in response to FCC concern—added 20 people to its news department to produce informational programs for young audiences. There was "In the News," the Saturday-morning series "30 Minutes," "What's an Election All About?" and "What's Congress All About?" And don't forget the hourlong Saturday morning "Children's Film Festival" and "Captain Kangaroo" weekdays. With deregulation in the 1980s, however, those 20 newspeople were gone and all those shows were canceled. In comments to the FCC at the time, CBS described one of its new children's offerings as dealing with "recognizable human beings in basic situations rather than the way-out world of the traditional animated cartoon." Curious, Action for Children's Television checked out this claim and monitored an episode that concerned the capture of a frozen caveman who chases the main character's friends, each trying to capture the other, until the caveman falls into a giant clam tank and is discovered to be a professor intent on stealing another scientist's invention.

By late 1981, children's television rule-making had disappeared from the FCC agenda. When the Commission's 1983 docket was closed in December 1983, "both the overall amount and creative quality of regularly scheduled children's programming were at one of the lowest levels in the history of television programming," commented Bruce Watkins in the *Yale Law & Policy Review.* My assessment at the time was that the FCC had left a giant lump of coal in the holiday stockings of all American children, while providing a great Christmas gift for the television industry.

Passage of the 1990 Children's Television Act was hailed as the beginning of true compliance and integrity in children's television programming. But a 1992 FCC report on industry compliance found that stations were claiming "The Jetsons," "Super Mario Brothers," "Leave It to Beaver," "G.I. Joe," "Smurfs" and a raft of similar fare as "educational" programming.

"If their lawyers weren't drunk, they must be sick," I suggested.

"Not necessarily," *Time* pointed out. "Regulators in the Reagan administration once tried to cut funds to school lunch programs by classifying catsup as a vegetable."

Perception is everything.

What seems abundantly clear in 1994 is that almost all of U.S. commercial television producers are still concentrating on how they can benefit from children, instead of how *they* can benefit children. This mind-set is particularly offensive in view of the dire needs of American children in the 1990s: one in four of TV's youngest viewers is poor; one in five is at risk of becoming a teen parent; one in seven is likely to drop out of school; half of all U.S. children born this year will live in single-parent households before they reach age 18; half of all working women in this country—20 million—have children under the age of 6. The needs exist.

As I said, broadcasters don't seem to understand how to obey the Children's Television Act and find the concept of educational programming difficult to grasp. But for goodness' sake, how hard is it to differentiate between "Superman" and "Sesame Street," between "Ninja Turtles" and "Nickelodeon"?

Broadcasters who want to ignore the mandate of the Children's Television Act also argue that they can't afford to air more than an hour a week of educational programming—up from 30 minutes in 1991. The law does not specify a required amount of children's programming; the National Association of Broadcasters, in its 1991 "Service to Children's Television Idea Book," demonstrates that it should. "While the amount of 'specifically designed' programming each station airs will vary according to its circumstances," the NAB "Idea Book" points out, "many private-practice broadcast lawyers have voiced the opinion that they will counsel their clients to air at least a weekly half-hour of educational and informational programs for children."

I would like to propose two alternative solutions to this long-standing confusion among commercial broadcasters as to what constitutes children's educational programming, and the equally thorny puzzle of how much airtime they have to devote to it.

One option might be to have the FCC adopt a four-point plan to govern quality and amounts of TV programming for children:

1. Each station shall air seven hours per week of "core" programs specifically designed to educate children. To qualify, these programs shall be at least 30 minutes long, aired only between 7 a.m. and 10 p.m.
2. Each station shall specify which target age group the program is designed to serve: preschool-age (2–5), school-age (6–11) or teen-age (12–16). If an examination of the categories in license renewal applications indicates that an age group is underserved by "core" programs, the FCC should promulgate additional guidelines to equalize service.
3. Stations shall provide a description of the educational goal for each "core" program, how the program is designed to meet this goal, and an evaluation of the program's effectiveness. This information shall be part of the broadcaster's public file. (The FCC should encourage efforts to make this information broadly available.)
4. Each station shall identify time and day "core" programs air and announce pre-emptions.

If this suggestion is found too cumbersome, an alternative might be a legislative solution that would relieve commercial broadcasters of the burden of deciding what is educational fare and finding the time in a busy broadcast day to air it.

There does exist one broadcast entity that provides a rich menu of programs designed to excite kids' minds and imaginations. The Public Broadcasting Service, an institution that had barely begun when I first came before the FCC, has made television learning in school and at home a high adventure with its now-classic teaching shows "Mr. Rogers' Neighborhood" and "Sesame Street," and "Long Ago & Far Away," "3-2-1 Contact" and, more recently, "Where in the World Is Carmen Sandiego?" Especially given its limited resources, public broadcasting's record in serving young audiences is remarkable for the array of choices it offers to children of various ages and for its willingness to tackle difficult topics and make them understandable to kids.

Maybe the FCC should relieve commercial broadcasters of their burdensome public-service obligation to children. Since the mechanism exists in the form of PBS to produce and deliver high-quality programming that actually benefits kids—a function for which commercial broadcasters have demonstrated both indifference and ineptitude—perhaps in the interests of cultivating the citizenry, the government should step in to ensure it happens. Why not charge the TV industry a very small percentage of its revenues—say, one-half of 1 percent—and allocate it to PBS, which knows how to do programs that educate children? I believe a reasonable amount is $100 million a year, which in fact is less than half of 1 percent of the broadcast TV industry revenues.

As Chief Justice Warren Burger wrote, "A broadcaster seeks and is granted the free and exclusive use of a limited and valuable part of the public domain; when he accepts that franchise, it is burdened by enforceable public obligations. A newspaper can be operated at the whim or caprice of its owners; a broadcast station cannot."

The issue of broadcasters' public-service responsibilities to the society that accords them use of the limited over-the-air channels available has been contested since the first Quaker Oats boxes were converted into radios. Decades later, commercial station service to young audiences is still capricious at best. The good news—if there is any—is that the current inhabitants of the White House have put the health and education of America's children at the center of their concerns. Perhaps that will result in some real and lasting improvement in how television's potential is used.

Peggy Charren, founder of Action for Children's Television, is a visiting scholar in Harvard University's Graduate School of Education.

4

Why Kids Hate Educational TV

Patricia Aufderheide

You don't have to get up early too many Saturday mornings with the kids before you're convinced that there's not much educational and informational programming for children on commercial broadcast television. And, by and large, what is there isn't very inspiring. What was Newton Minow's line? The Vast Wasteland is perhaps vastest on Saturday mornings.

And yet, you find yourself muttering as you start the coffeemaker, how hard can it really be to make programs that will do more for kids than convince them to buy brand-name paraphernalia—G.I. Joe guns! X-Men dolls! Mighty Morphin Power Rangers birthday paper plates!—or take them on a mind-numbing, action-packed roller-coaster ride of slapstick?

OK, you think, maybe you're just not looking in the right place, because Saturday morning is playtime, after all, not schooltime. But you won't find much that's educational or informational on during the week either. In fact, it's scary—*most* of the good-for-you stuff airs on the weekend.

Well, you tell yourself, grabbing the TV schedule, maybe you're just not watching at the right time. And you'd be right, because you probably can't wake the kids up early enough—before 8 or even 7 a.m.—to see television's substantial minority of good-for-you kidshows.

But most probably, like most of us, you don't really think much of anything about kids' TV. The farthest most of us get is an offhand discussion with an exercised conscience: "I watched a lot of TV, and it didn't hurt me. I think." Or, "Television is a part of our culture that they'd better understand." Or, "They don't watch that much, anyway.

And if I didn't have the TV while I'm making dinner I'd go crazy."
Most of us don't think of television as a potential educational resource
at all; we think of television the way it's come to us over the years—
entertainment, cheerfully complacent in its vulgarity and its bottom-
line objectives. And if it was good enough for us, then...

That wasn't Peggy Charren's reaction when she began her campaign
for good kids' television three decades ago, founding Action for
Children's Television and striking the fear of God into network executives. Charren thought it was an outrage that a civilized society would
let television, when it wasn't just plain ignoring children, do nothing
more than hawk junk to kids, sitting ducks for pitchmen. It's hard to
dispute that view. Television may not be the only influence on our
children's lives, but it's an insidiously captivating one. As Peggy Charren
has pointed out for years and years, broadcasters may be in a for-profit
business, but they're also licensees of the public airwaves and required
by law to serve the public interest.

Charren's dogged persistence finally pushed the Children's Television Act of 1990 into existence, despite the objections of a Republican
president. It was to be her organization's swan song; she retired in 1993,
folding ACT as she went. The legislation says that broadcast stations
(the part of the TV industry directly beholden to Congress for licenses)
must carry educational and informational kids' programming, and must
show the Federal Communications Commission at licensing-renewal
time what they have done for kids.

The Republican-led FCC at the time the law was passed wrote the
kind of wink-wink regulations that made it easy for broadcasters not to
take the law seriously. It wasn't until Charren's successors, the Washington-based Center for Media Education, motivated legislators and regulators in the new Clinton administration to re-examine the market and
the law that the 1990 Act took on substance.

One of the things that CME, in conjunction with Georgetown
University's Center for Public Representation, did to insist on compliance was to study broadcasters' license renewals and to publicize the
sillier things they found. Some stations claimed, for instance, that shows
like "Leave It to Beaver," "The Jetsons" and "G.I. Joe" constituted
educational fare. Publicizing those claims put egg on broadcasters'
faces. If they hated the public shaming and the attention it brought
from Congress and the Clinton-era FCC, they also decided by late

1992 and early 1993 to start putting on programs they could defend without looking ridiculous.

In early 1994, CME asked me to look at the commercial broadcast marketplace for educational and informational children's programs over the previous year to see how broadcasters had risen to the challenge. I talked to nearly 50 providers of programming and key decision-makers at the four major networks to get a better understanding of how the process works.

It was pretty easy to figure out what happened in 1993. Everybody who had a program remotely plausible as educational or informational—or, as they instantly became known, "FCC-friendly," a term that demonstrates just how cynical people inside the industry were about the law—immediately hauled it to a market or took out an ad. The trades compiled comprehensive lists of these shows, more than 75, by mid-summer '93.

Stations went shopping and made sure they had at least one show they could wave before the FCC. If they were affiliates, they might get it through a network, since each network had at least one "FCC-friendly" offering of its own (CBS's science show "Beakman's World"; NBC's teen show on careers, "Name Your Adventure"; ABC's science offering, "Cro"; PBS's geography show "Where in the World Is Carmen Sandiego?" which belatedly replaced "Bobby's World" and its prosocial values) cleared by their own lawyers for the season. Or affiliates might buy something from a syndicator.

The syndicators' deals virtually all worked on what's known as barter: A syndicator splits the advertising time with the local station, with the local station collecting revenues from ads it can place, usually local, and the syndicator receiving revenues from the national ad time, potentially lucrative if enough stations in enough markets place the program at a good enough time for children to watch. Barter deals in kids' programming really began to flourish in 1984, when the FCC lifted its strictures against program-length commercials like "He-Man" and, in short order, "Strawberry Shortcake," "My Little Pony" and "Transformers." That was when every gimmick promoter in the country leaped at the chance to use television to sell to kids.

Of course, the concept of using shows as advertisement was not new. Not one aging baby boomer who can remember Mickey Mouse Club watches ("Good things come in small packages") and the product hyping on "Romper Room" in the old days will be shocked by the notion. In fact, this was what had brought forth the FCC stricture in the first place. But that was the pre-Reagan administration, before it was common knowledge that, as Reagan-appointed FCC head Mark Fowler put it, the public interest is what the public is interested in, and the market would answer society's needs as well as anything was going to.

The 1993 market in educational and informational programming for kids arrived as if to show the Reagan ideologues, if belatedly, that there are some areas of life that the marketplace simply does not provide for very well.

The problem with the barter notion for educational and informational kids' programming was that without a serious licensing sideline—a "My Little Pony," "Transformer" or "Smurf"—the whole thing was a gamble on hitting around 75 percent to 80 percent of the nation's markets (including the top three, New York, Los Angeles and Chicago) in order to make national ad revenue pay the rest of the costs. To do that syndicators needed lots of stations, and good time slots in each. But the best time slots were mostly taken up by shows aimed at other and more lucrative demographics, by sports, and by other kidshows with more money to bid because they had the promise that kids would buy mountains of junk if the show simply aired.

Things were a little better at the networks, but even there affiliated stations had better things to do with their best time slots than to give them to the educational and informational fare. And networks themselves sometimes placed those programs in spots virtually guaranteed to be pre-empted. "Beakman's World," for instance, was pre-empted during much of the first half of 1994 on the West Coast because of CBS's Olympics and other sports coverage.

When good kidshows were placed at good times, they got good ratings, but not as much money overall as product-related programs could.

What is fascinating about this dance is not just what broadcasters and programmers say, but the way they say it. Many of the people I talked to clearly liked kids and were fascinated by the challenge of engaging them seriously. But others talked as if the consciousness, the curiosity, the passion to learn inherent in children—the same kids who one day will vote on Social Security and medical care—were either fodder for their money-making machines or simply nothing to worry about.

Take Howard France, a syndicator who had picked up a kids' fitness show: "In December 1992, a producer brought 'Scramble' to us," France said. "He was in it for the money—it was a unique merchandising opportunity, because of Randall Cunningham, a famous football player. [Note: *"Unique merchandising opportunity" means syndicators can sell a lot of toys, doo-dads, placemats and key rings branded with the name of the show and star.*]

"He [the producer] said, 'Without TV, I'm nothing.'" [Note: *The TV show itself is the ad for the stuff.*]

"I said, 'It'll be a difficult show to clear [i.e., *to get enough markets to make a national-reach claim to advertisers*]. Maybe we can clear it by touting it as FCC-friendly.'"

France continued, "This was all the rage among distributors, because the station wants to put on "Morphin" and cartoons that make them money. Educational TV doesn't make any money historically. Is a show FCC-friendly? How do you know? The FCC so far says, 'We won't define it, but we'll know it when we see it.'

"The show has been canceled but it was 72 percent [clearance] at its peak. It was canceled in December. Why? Because nobody watched it," France said. "If you've got a "Mighty Morphin" with a 6 or a 7 rating, you can make a decent amount of money, but in kids' TV you can't expect that kind of breakout—you have to hope to do a 2 rating. There's not much money to be made there. There has to be another angle, dolls or lunch buckets or something.

"A big contributing factor was the time of the show. Stations reserved their best time periods for the shows most important to them, cartoons. They had this government incentive, these threats, to put this kind of programming on, but they don't give this programming the best time period," France said. "Also the show had weaknesses."

Howard France had done an admirable job of demonstrating the kind of match-made-in-hell created by the FCC's wink-wink kids' TV regulation. A guy whose highest ambition was to move products stamped with his celebrity's logo had found a distributor savvy enough to know that stations needed something "FCC-friendly" enough to convince the Commission it had fulfilled minimal obligations for license renewal. Everyone was depending on the rules staying loose, and on a shared contempt for the spirit of the law.

"The FCC is telling you you have to put boring TV on—the primary focus has to be educational, not entertaining," France complained. "You know kids, they don't want to go to school all week. If they don't want to watch it, who's gonna make 'em? The government can't pass a law to make people watch shows."

This is familiar ground. Practically everyone I talked to for this study—especially all the network people—managed to work into their rap a discussion of how kids don't want to be educated with television, and how no one can force a person to watch boring programming. For instance, take Jenny Trias, head of children's programming at ABC. "I've done focus groups over my 15 years here," Trias said, "and I will always remember that one little boy said, 'I go to school Monday to Friday. Saturday morning is *my* time.' The most important thing should be entertainment, and if we can add educational elements, it's icing on top of the cake."

Over and over distributors and programmers say that, sad as it might be to admit, the problem is that kids just don't want to learn when they aren't in school: They just want diversion and distraction.

This attitude seems to assume that kids enter predestined into the dismal work-vs.-leisure-time mode their parents grew into. It assumes that learning is, and should be, the same thing as schooling. It pretends that kids don't learn from entertainment. And it overstates the case, as if not making *as much* money as other programming is the same as not making *any* money. Such thinking flies in the face of evidence like "Sesame Street" and other hits from the Children's Television Workshop, which has ridden public television to financial success of its own (including a major business in licensed products), and the distinguished histories of "Captain Kangaroo" and "Mr. Wizard," which managed not to lose money while also speaking to children's curiosity. It shrugs off the promotional and brand-identity value of a feature like "Schoolhouse Rock," whose jingles remain indelibly imprinted in many parents' minds today.

Nonetheless, this sentiment is so widely accepted that TV people recite it semi-automatically, explaining the obvious to an outsider. That's how Howard France said it. France had just finished explaining in some detail how he had successfully taken up space and time in a station's schedule with low-budget programming whose objective wasn't to teach anything or even to entertain, but merely to sell. No wonder kids don't watch the stuff.

Not that quality can't happen. "Cro," "Beakman" and "Where in the World Is Carmen Sandiego?" are all examples of network shows with production values and some investment in research into the educational side of the show. And when they're on in good time slots, these offerings get respectable ratings. In syndication, there's "Bill Nye the Science Guy," which, like "Cro," used about a million dollars of taxpayer money in grants to do that research. Bill Nye also launched the show at a public TV station, thus adding to the public investment in his program (which Disney is now syndicating). In local programming, look at KCNC-TV in Denver, whose "News for Kids" is a snappy and self-possessed little news show that depends on a low, low budget, but has the backing of the station and in-house resources to accomplish much more than what most stations are doing.

But even when a show gets a decent budget and maybe even network support, the schedule is usually still a problem. And when a show doesn't air when kids can see it, ratings plummet and the old self-fulfilling prophecy kicks in: Kids just "don't want to watch it."

What's keeping the stations from running shows like this at good times and promoting them the way they do other shows is that nobody's making them do it, and there are more lucrative options. For people who are trying in good faith to make interesting programs for kids, often against great odds, this can be completely crazy-making. "I work out of a station, so I understand the dollars and cents," said Kent Takano, producer of the now-defunct teen show "Scratch," "but when you see how some stations treat it, you want to say, 'Why take it at all?'"

Squire Rushnell, an independent producer who was head of children's programming at ABC through the "Schoolhouse Rock" era of the 1970s, explained why he's discouraged in this market, so concerned with licensing deals. "You need to have a program that's paid for, but then you also need to get stations to clear it," he sighs. "'Sonic the Hedgehog' doesn't make it because it's a good program; it makes it because Sega is willing to put in extra dollars for advertising and promotion. So if you're going, say, to a station in Chicago, the company has to be ready to put more advertising dollars into that market [buy additional advertising] because otherwise, the station might go with a Hasbro-related program."

Allen Bohbot, a plain-talking distributor of animated and action-oriented kids' programming ("Some people call it violence, I call it action.") confirms that paying for time slots, whether through pledging advertising to a station or other incentives, is now standard practice. "It's not a good practice, but it's reality," he said.

And, Bohbot says, it's not that he tries *not* to market educational programming—it just doesn't pay.

"The kids come home and the last thing they want to do is be educated," he says. "They want entertainment. It scares the daylights out of me. If I were a parent I'd be very concerned—not just what gets to the air but what succeeds.

"TV is mirroring what they see in their daily lives. I think we kid ourselves if we ignore that," he observed. "As things get worse and worse for kids in their daily lives, entertainment seems to follow. Disney ratings are down 55 percent in the last three years in some of the classic animated shows, but those animals are not real world. 'Mighty Morphin Power Rangers'—that seems more accepted, more like what they want.

"That doesn't make it right," Bohbot said. "Most of us are conscientious adults. We've done all kinds of shows like 'Gulliver's Travels,' and they're the lowest-rated shows we've ever had. The better return isn't on the socially acceptable program but on where the kids are glued to the set.

"Is it in the wrong direction? Yes. Is it where people are tuning in? Yes."

This jaded view of a descent into a social hell, lit dimly by the flickering action on the tube, might be expected from a syndicator, out on the do-or-die feeding frenzy of the business front lines of TV programming. But coming from someone like Bohbot, for whom programming is strictly business, not any kind of social quest, these gloomy comments paint a vivid picture of what anyone with educational/informational programming competes with in today's children's TV marketplace. Clearly, without help from regulators to shape and constrain market conditions, kids are unlikely to see the kind of programming the 1990 Act mandated.

Patricia Aufderheide is an associate professor in the School of Communication at the American University in Washington and a senior editor of In These Times *newspaper. This chapter is drawn from her research with the Center for Media Education on the aftermath of the 1990 Children's Television Act.*

5

Electronic Childhood

Ellen Wartella

My children are living an electronic childhood. And they are not alone. Channel surfing on cable, computer games, videos, e-mail and Internet are features of a world often alien to adults, but as familiar as the backyard to my sons, 11 and 6. As parents, teachers and television producers observe our children in this electronic world, we are both awed by their agility with media that sometimes intimidate us, and fearful of the ways those new media are changing the nature of children's lives and the society in which they grow up.

Indeed, concerns about the social effects of media on children and youth are echoed everywhere, and this shared worry can only accelerate as the marketplace for media products becomes ever more global and homogenized across national boundaries. Critics complain that young people spend too much time with media products that are too violent, commercialized and of inappropriate quality. But proponents of television, as well as champions of some of the newer interactive technologies such as video and computer, argue that such media enhance children's education.

Although several countries (such as France and Canada) limit importation of foreign films or television programs, a global cultural marketplace now exists in which media fare created in, say, Ireland, are marketed elsewhere in Europe as well as in the Americas, Asia and Australia. Throughout much of the global marketplace, the standards of aesthetic tastes or expectations for television dramatic content, films, popular music and videos are also increasingly homogenized. Like the armies of old, cultural products, created and distributed by multinational media conglomerates, now traverse industrialized democracies. And such a global international media market finds some of its most avid audiences among children.

What is this international electronic media environment for children?

In both Europe and the United States, children are heavy users of television and, increasingly, of all television programs accessed via the television set (i.e., videos, computer games). Children's television habits in Europe and the United States have been found to follow a similar pattern: Children are early users of television, showing a steady increase in viewing time from about age 2 until middle childhood (about age 8 or 9). Between the ages of 8 and 12, television viewing seems to level off at about two-and-three-quarter hours per day and then actually starts to decrease through adolescence, with the least amount of television viewing occurring among 14- to 19-year-olds, who watch about two hours per day.

But the TV set now makes available more than terrestrial television channels for children to watch: Cable, satellites and videocassettes have now made considerable inroads into children's viewing of over-the-air television. In the United States, more than 60 percent of households now have cable and nearly three-quarters have VCRs. The most recent statistics I have seen on video-game usage suggest that one out of every three U.S. homes has a video game. Personal computers and CD-ROMs are less common, being newer, more expensive technologies, but are increasingly widespread every year.

In Europe, video and satellite penetration is more variable across countries. In 1988–89, for instance, the proportion of Italian households with a video recording machine was 19 percent, but 54 percent in Great Britain. And, as in the United States, in Europe households with children are more likely to own a VCR than are households without children. One British industry report found in 1990 that 22 percent of the population aged 7 and over had watched video during the previous week. The frequency of satellite TV viewing lies somewhere between terrestrial TV use and video use.

Without question, children today grow up in much more media-rich households than their parents' and, importantly, with more uses for the television set.

What do we know about what children watch on television? It's mostly adult fare. Children do not by any means watch only programs intended specifically for them. Horst Stipp, director of social and development research at NBC, recently pointed out that U.S. commercial television executives are fully aware that America's children prefer situation comedies to children's educational programs. Stipp says most of the programs that U.S. children watch are neither specially created for children nor shown in what is known as children's TV time—Saturday mornings.

A second noteworthy characteristic of children's viewing is that it roams across a range of live-action and animated fare that appears on cable or in syndication on local stations, not just on America's four commercial over-the-air networks. A third factor worth noting is that not one educational children's television show appears in the top-viewed programs, although if we looked at the ratings for children aged 2 to 5 separately from those aged 6 to 11, "Sesame Street," a widely acclaimed educational program for preschoolers, would make that list.

These data are not unique to the United States. When examining the listings of the top 10 programs for children in Great Britain, Switzerland, West Germany, France and the Netherlands, the most popular shows are comedies, game shows and soap operas. While preschool-aged children may start watching television by attending to children's programs, by the time they reach age 6 or 7 they watch more adult fare than children's programming.

Clearly, part of the explanation of children's viewing preferences may be the range of choices offered. Certainly, in the United States, the diversity and variety of entertaining fare specifically produced for children is limited, even with a proliferation of media and channels. In a 1990 study, I examined the variety and diversity of children's programming available in one Midwestern community. The question raised was whether children had access to both over-the-air broadcasts, cable and videocassette rentals of children's programming and whether that content included a range of genres for children to watch. In particular, I was interested in gauging the extent to which children's offerings provided them with informational or educational options (a particular concern of American public policy-makers).

We found that while the children in this community lived in homes with a variety of media available, including cable television and videocassette recorders, neither traditional broadcast television nor videocassette recorders provided much diversity of content for children. There were few informational or educational children's shows on broadcast television at the time, and most of those were dominated by toy-related animated programs—"Teenage Mutant Ninja Turtles" and the like. Similarly, most of the video rental fare was either adult-oriented or the same animated TV programs. The major exceptions to these were recycled Disney movies and some public broadcasting educational series such as "Sesame Street." Only households with cable were offered both variety and diversity of children's programming: Channels such as Nickelodeon, a commercial enterprise, offer a range of programming genres, quiz shows, game shows, drama, animated cartoons and variety shows, thus adding to the diversity of children's program options.

Since that 1990 study, there is now more competition in production of children's television and more program diversity in the United States. Much of this has been prompted by passage of the Children's Television Act of 1990, intended to increase the amount of educational and informational broadcast television programming available to children. Two of its provisions are important for the future of American children's television: that broadcasters must provide television programming that serves the educational and informational needs of children, and that, if they do not, broadcasters may be held accountable in license reviews every five years; second, the Act established a National Endowment for Children's Educational Television, a vehicle through which new programming ventures can be funded.

In addition to that important step, Congress in summer 1993 enacted the National Ready to Learn Act, which sets the goal of having all U.S. children prepared and ready to learn when they enter public school, and includes the use of television as part of the mandate. This year, money was funneled into public television to achieve this goal. Indeed, a few months ago, the U.S. public television system announced a renewed commitment to air an expanded block of nine hours a day of educational and informational children's programming this fall.

It may well be that the United States is approaching a renaissance in television programming for children. Even this year, one can point to a much larger diversity of programming genres for children on U.S. commercial television than was present a few years ago, in particular, renewed interest in science programs and quiz and game shows. The impact of privatized television on Europe's far more developed tradition of public broadcasting is less clear, although increasing amounts of U.S.

animated children's programming now appear worldwide, so content improvements in the United States may have a positive global impact.

Concern about what children see and assimilate from television and videos is rooted in an assumption that the impact of television and other media is heavily determined by their content. Two aspects of content that have received most research and comment involve the violence and commercialization of much of commercial TV fare.

Violence in the media has been a topic for public debate and academic research since the film era in the 1920s, at least in the United States, where media violence has always seemed of more concern than in other areas of the world. In part this may be because American cultural products seem more violent than those of other countries. Yet, increasingly, media violence also transverses the globe, as the recent British outcry over "video nasties" demonstrates. Several major reviews of the predominantly U.S. research on violence effects have been issued over the past several years, converging on the conclusion that media violence is one environmental factor contributing to the maintenance of a stable pattern of aggressive behavior in children and adults. However, these studies conclude, media violence does constitute a threat to public health.

Partly because of such research and partly because of the political pressures to "do something" about violence in American life, U.S. cultural industries are responding. This year, the networks and the cable industry announced mechanisms to self-regulate their violent content, including the establishment of independent monitors to measure the amount of violence on television. In May 1994, the National Cable Television Association announced that it would contract with a consortium of four universities under the auspices of Mediascope (a not-for-profit organization in Hollywood organized to bring academics and industry people together around social issues of concern) to conduct TV violence monitoring over the next three years.

The second issue of public concern about television—commercialization—is exacerbated by the rise of privatized television in Europe and elsewhere in competition with public broadcasting, which has raised the stakes of a commercialized childhood. Around the world, for example, children now have access to the "Teenage Mutant Ninja Turtles" (or "Teenage Mutant Hero Turtles," as they are known in Great Britain) via television, video, books, interactive video games, movies and a whole host of toy products, comic books, clothing and children's furnishings. Programs that link television characters to toy products—termed program-length commercials in the United States—are of increasing concern around the globe.

The fact that television program characters are created with an eye toward their marketing potential as toys or other consumer items is only part of an entire marketing strategy that has evolved over a decade. Starting from the premise that children like the familiar and recognizable, the creation of children's programming (once based on children's books or films) is an elaborate manifestation of providing children with something familiar. Today, simultaneous production of a children's TV show and its toy-related characters is an assumed part of the package, with the relationship between media and merchandise reinforced via product licensing (such as for backpacks, sheets, towels, clothing and lunch boxes), cereal products (e.g., breakfast boxes featuring "Ghostbusters" and "The Addams Family"), character appearances at shopping malls and holiday events, movie appearances ("Batman: The Animated Movie" is based on Fox's kidshow, which in turn was issued after the success of the live-action [adult] "Batman" films), and, of course, a host of new-technology toys including arcade and home video games, story tapes and home-computer software. These characters and products range widely around the world—it is difficult to escape purple dinosaurs or talking fire engines anywhere.

What is emerging is unique to the new electronic age, what Marsha Kinder in her book on video games calls a "supersystem: a network of interrelated narrative texts or media products constructed around a pop cultural figure or group of figures." In addition to the Turtles, there are the characters from the "Star Wars" movies, the Simpsons, the Smurfs, the Muppets of "Sesame Street," Batman and, born-again through Hollywood's magic and eagerness to recycle proven vehicles, the Flintstones. Sometimes, pop cultural icons are real people too— Madonna, Michael Jackson and even the (apparently) dead Elvis Presley. "In order to be a supersystem," writes Kinder, "the network must cut across several modes of image production; must appeal to diverse generations, classes, ethnic subcultures, who in turn are targeted with diverse strategies; must foster 'collectibility' through a proliferation of related products; and must undergo a sudden increase in commodification, the success of which reflexively becomes a 'media event' that dramatically accelerates the growth curve of the system's commercial success."

Indeed, the notion of "interactive" media is a double entendre—not only are users interacting with the images on screens, but one media outlet is interacting with others in one large consumerist dance. And children—even preschoolers—are at its center, by being educated to become part of the consumer group of children around the world (and certainly at their preschools and in their neighborhoods) who together can play with the Turtles, Barney or other cultural icons.

If I am engaging the old arguments about marketplace constraints on the quality of cultural products, I do so with an awareness of the higher stakes involved in global markets saturated with a handful of cultural supersystems. The concern, of course, is that marketing will outweigh any concern with aesthetics. Moreover, I fear we are developing a generation of cynical consumers.

Beyond the pitfalls of commercialization, a media system of interrelated products has implications for the potential of new electronic media to enhance children's lives. Indeed, there are high hopes that the active nature of children's interactions with video games and computers, as well as the other newer electronic audio and video products, will help children learn about the world and themselves.

Many of the production principles that have governed children's television are being carried over into other interactive media. And no wonder. Many of the same production houses are moving into multiple technologies for delivering media products and, as discussed, cultural icons across media are often part of the same supersystem. These principles are rooted in observations of what engages and interests children as media users.

One principle that should be incorporated into production of all children's media is that repetition is a key to both educating and entertaining children. Just as children like to have the same stories read to them over and over, they enjoy the same television programs and videos. Repetition is not just important but essential to video games, since practice leads to mastery. Repetition both entertains and hones new skills: In video games as in life, once children learn to master one sort of obstacle, whenever it arises again, they are prepared.

A second principle is that children want recognizable characters and stories. And the supersystem of cultural production ensures that children can find favorite characters across a range of media technologies. In the future, recycling children's stories from television to video to CD-ROM to computer games and back again is likely to be the norm, not the exception. As discussed, this principle is very effective in developing marketing strategies for children, but only in the short term: Supersystems of image marketing quickly lead to cynicism among the older child audience members.

A third principle is that gender differences survive into this new electronic world. The common assumption among U.S. children's TV producers, for instance, is that boys like fast-paced action, adventure and superheroes, while girls take to fantasy, soft, cuddly characters and slower-paced television. Action, and often violence (good vs. evil, heroic feats, technical wizardry and male-dominated characters) are all marks of boys' television best typified by the Ninja Turtles' success. Girls' programming is dominated by sugary-sweet programs about cute, doll-like characters who demonstrate good pro-social qualities of caring and helpfulness (e.g., Ariel in "The Little Mermaid"). This expectation of male bias towards action and superheroes has carried over from movies and television into the video-game industry. As Kinder reports, the vast majority of video-game players are boys; when surveyed, both girls and boys as young as 5 and 6 see video games as more appropriate for boys than girls. Manufacturers see that, of course, so it is no surprise that current video-game products are more boy-oriented than girl-oriented, which clearly may have repercussions if such interactive media do, as some observers claim, have an impact on children's cognitive development.

Fourth, an implication of new media for children is that the nature of the visual-spatial interactivity of media such as video games and computers may have a positive impact on cognitive development. Psychologist Patricia Greenfield, for instance, suggests in her book *Mind and Media* that video-game playing does offer important cognitive benefits. The very structure of video games fosters the use of an inductive reasoning process, provides a means of verifying hypotheses, improves eye-hand coordination and the processing of visual information from multiple perspectives and helps develop skills in iconic-spatial representation. But video games tend to be based on boy-oriented television and video narratives; if video games are a gateway into greater comfort with computer use, then girls quite clearly are disadvantaged in entering the increasingly computerized work world. When transplanted to newer technologies, the gendered world of children's television may have serious consequences for future generations of workers.

On the other hand, there is something of a blurring of age distinctions in children's use of interactive technologies. I have observed boys as young as 3 and 4 rally round my 11-year-old when he's playing with his video games. In many ways, video games, computers and other new media can draw children and adolescents together around their interactive technology; sometimes only parents feel left out. Part of this observation is rooted in the way television is programmed for children. If, for instance, children "watch up"—that is, watch the programs that attract older siblings—it is no surprise that programmers seek to develop shows for an elastic age group of 5- to 13-year-olds. One beneficial result of this blurring of age-group interest in new media is that it may indeed lead to children of different ages, perhaps even with adults, gathering round interactive technologies together. I know that my children and their friends like to play video games together, the group watching while one tries his hand at the game. Contrary to many fears that video games and computers will lead to greater individual and social isolation, it may be that at least some of these technologies have inherent social aspects that have been thus far ignored.

The potential for new interactive media to change the nature of children's leisure time is enormous. Already, children are faced with a dizzying array of high-tech activities that fill their electronic childhoods, as well as with traditional printed media. Harnessing the potential of these old and new media to create entertaining as well as educationally beneficial cultural products, and to do so without further commercialization of our youth, is the challenge we all face. If history is a guide, great expectations of the transformatory power of new media to wonderfully enhance children's cognitive and emotional lives probably will fall short. On the other hand, if we do produce the very best products possible, perhaps those goals will move closer. In much of the world, children already live an electronic childhood. Can we make it a healthy, safe and caring one?

Ellen Wartella, dean of the College of Communication at the University of Texas-Austin and a 1985–86 Freedom Forum Media Studies Center fellow, adapted this chapter from her remarks at The Cologne Conference, Germany, June 1994.

II
Covering Children

6

Symposium II

Jana Eisenberg

Children and the Media returns here to our "symposium" of snapshot interviews with a broad range of experts who understand well issues of children and the media, to set the scene for this section of essays on how U.S. media cover children.

To open this section, six knowledgeable sources—a journalist-author, a scholar, a producer, a publisher, an entertainer and a professor—join forces to discuss how the media cover kids.

Alex Kotlowitz, author and former Wall Street Journal *reporter covering children:*

The media tend to view children growing up in urban poverty as either victims or perpetrators. When the Chicago police recently launched a manhunt to capture 11-year-old Robert Sandifer—who allegedly killed a 14-year-old girl—public officials demanded tougher treatment of juvenile offenders. When it was learned that Robert had been executed by his own gang, the outcry shifted: Social service agencies and his family had failed him.

Portraying children like Robert only as victims of poverty and violence does them a disservice. It suggests that they are destined to failure. We overlook the fact that they are still just children. They, too, shoot marbles, go on dates, win spelling bees and keep diaries. Some find places and people where and with whom they feel safe and taken care of.

If we portray children only as perpetrators, we forget what it means to be a child: vulnerable, impressionable and needy. For many of these kids, a single act of violence may be the event around which all other experiences revolve, an event many of them, like soldiers returning from combat, will relive again and again. We also then shy away from making institutions like the police, the courts, the schools and the church accountable.

As reporters, our biggest challenge is a straightforward one—to put a human face on the children living in our ravaged cities. To recognize their strengths as well as their frailties. To understand their fears, aspirations and anger. Writing about children requires what our profession treasures least: patience in reporting, complexity in storytelling.

Gerald Lesser, professor of education and psychology, Harvard University; chairman of boards of advisers and consultants, Children's Television Workshop:

Children need more diversity than they are getting from the media. Despite the proliferation of channels, it's just more of the same. You can mean different things by "diversity": Are we providing enough programs for kids of different ages? Are we providing enough programs that are both educational and entertaining? Do we have enough programs that invite children to think about things they never would have thought about without the benefit of the media? That would be true diversity.

What can we do in this current environment? A very specific answer is to enforce the Children's Television Act of 1990, which calls on stations, as a condition for license renewal, "to serve the informational and educational needs of children." The FCC has made weak efforts to enforce that provision, which has been law for four years.

There's an equity issue involved in this as well. The new technologies are available to folks who are better off. But my inclination is to work in broadcast television for the simple reason that it's available to everybody. We know that 98.5 percent of households in this country have television sets. I'm not disparaging efforts toward developing new media, but approximately one-third of our population does not have cable, and many more are lacking other new technologies. Broadcast television still has the best opportunity—and has had for a long time, even though it hasn't acted on it—to reach low-income families effectively.

Linda Ellerbee, president, Lucky Duck Productions; executive producer, writer and host of Nickelodeon's "Nick News":

Until recently, if a kid wanted news about the world, he had the evening news. Evening newscasts do not serve kids and are not meant to. The primary thing wrong with the evening news for kids is that it presumes prior knowledge. On our shows we constantly give the context. For example, if we are doing a story on a town that is going under because a military base closes, we try to explain a single-industry town. And since the end of the Cold War caused the military base to close, we stop and do 10 minutes on the Cold War. Otherwise it doesn't mean anything.

Kids also tell us how mad they get at the news' portrayal of them. Overwhelmingly, when you see kids on the news, it's because they are in trouble. If you got your opinion of kids solely from the news, you would think that they were all either criminals or victims.

Kids all agree that the scariest thing on television is the news. And when we ask them if watching violence on TV makes them violent, they aren't sure, but they are sure that watching violence makes them afraid.

The solution to the abundance of commercials—and for much of what we are talking about here—is media literacy. You have to sit down and watch TV with kids and educate them about it. They need to know what editing is, that something was left out. They need to know what ads are really doing: Are they selling toothpaste or popularity? It is not enough any more to teach kids how to read and write. They must be media literate. Otherwise, television, rather than being a tool, is going to be some mysterious power in their lives.

Adam Linter, editor in chief and publisher, Tomorrow's Morning, *a Los Angeles weekly newspaper for kids:*

There's a lot going on for 8- to 14-year-olds. They are sponges. They have a lot of information but not a lot of knowledge. They are very nervous about what's going to be there when they grow up. Kids at this stage are starting to share and interrelate experiences; many are activists, fully tuned in and wanting to do something to make a difference.

In *Tomorrow's Morning,* we have a kid's stock column. It's a way to directly relate to the world—show them the companies they support by wearing their sneakers, watching their TV shows, going to their movies, drinking their soft drinks. Kids influence $140 billion in spending in this country.

The fourth grade is around when kids should make the shift from learning to read to reading to learn. About half never manage that shift. Newspaper readership is declining in general, but a newspaper is something that, unlike textbooks, is current. If you try to get kids to start reading one at the high school level, it's already too late. And most traditional children's publications have no credibility with kids because they are watered down to avoid offense. You can't talk down to kids. They are smart enough to recognize what message you are trying to deliver. If you deliver the right message, they will take it and act on it.

Raffi, singer/songwriter, family entertainer and activist:

Visual media channel society's behavior to children in their formative and impressionable years. The African adage says, "It takes the whole village to raise a child." Remembering that the duty of village elders is to show children where and how they belong in the tribe, what do our media show and tell?

Kids' heroes are Barbie and Ken, rock stars and wrestlers—slim pickings as role models. Children have an inner timetable of growth and discovery. They need to exercise their imaginations, but, instead, they are fed a diet of pre-fab images and quick-edit storms geared to sell things.

Money, the symbolic reward of our endeavors, has been elevated above the meaning of what we do. Symbols have replaced emotions, the bank has replaced the temple, and notoriety has supplanted integrity. We stand to lose the rich diversity of countless tribes and many paths that are humanity's heritage. Unless the teachings of the global culture emphasize and promote health and evolution, we will continue to wrongly favor looks over feeling, data over experience, and nutrient-thin foods that contain toxins over nutritious fare.

Love is the prime nutrient in healthy human development—the nurturing, demonstrative, appropriate, feeling love that children need to grow whole. Young children need to interact more with people and nature, not machines. Relationships and interdependence weave the web of life. When the elders have reviewed their priorities and once again found their way, the media will reflect a profound reassurance to our young.

Samuel Freedman, assistant professor and faculty adviser to the Fellowship Program for Children and the News, Columbia University Graduate School of Journalism:

Children's issues are getting more coverage in a more distinct way than they have ever gotten before. But we're in a political climate where a social issue, in order to attract attention, has to be cast as a middle-class issue. A way of covering children's issues is beginning in which any kind of stress or tension in the family (i.e., problems the parent has balancing work and child care) is treated as a morally equivalent problem to the problems of millions of kids growing up in inner cities, where childhood as we conceive of it no longer exists.

People on newspapers and magazines and in electronic media feel that in order to draw readers' attention to *those* issues, they've got to wrap it up with the anxiety kids have about going to summer camp, or whether the TV show "Barney" is a good influence. Anyone who is worried about whether "Barney" is a bad influence on their kid has a luxury problem.

An emerging children's issue is what I call the "commodification" of children, one aspect of which is that the acquisition of a child now has a commercial element to it. There's something dreadful about babies becoming a new third world export, yet another natural resource to be pillaged by wealthy countries. And every time I see a story about it, it's almost always a first-person account of someone who adopted a baby in Yugoslavia or Korea or wherever and just how wonderful it was to have finally gotten a child.

7

From Unseen and Unheard to Kidsbeat

Cathy Trost

For years, the children's beat was the Rodney Dangerfield of American newsrooms—it got no respect. Covering politics or City Hall was the journalist's dream job, and few wanted to get sidetracked into the low-status, soft-news backwater of kids.

Fast forward to the 1990s. The *Philadelphia Inquirer*'s Pulitzer-prize winning reporter John Woestendiek returns from a domestic assignment to cover children's issues. Robert F. Kennedy Journalism Award-winner Jane Daugherty captains one of the most ambitious projects on children ever launched, the *Detroit Free Press*'s hard-hitting "Children First" team, reporting on children's problems and their solutions. *Washington Post* national political correspondent Paul Taylor drops his prestigious beat to cover children's issues before taking a foreign assignment. The *Chicago Tribune* mobilizes 75 reporters, 35 photographers and graphic artists and almost the entire editing staff on a yearlong series on children and violence.

After decades of neglect, the media are finally beginning to cover children and families as serious topics, pushed by audience interest and growing national concern about the welfare of children. New print and broadcast projects focusing on children are popping up everywhere, in media markets both big and small. The kidsbeat is on the front lines of pivotal national issues, and on the front pages.

Kidsbeats are finally getting some respect. But, as Mr. Dangerfield might say, "I've got some good news and some bad news."

The good news is that editors are increasingly recognizing that the complex forces shaping children's lives today are front-burner issues for their readers, viewers and listeners, and are critical links to America's future as a competitive nation.

The bad news is that there are still plenty of barriers to good coverage, and too much of the reporting about children is still shallow or sensational.

When the University of Maryland's Casey Journalism Center for Children and Families recently surveyed the media's coverage of children's issues, we found that reporting power is often sparse and thinly scattered, with too few bodies to cover the range of critical issues facing children and families. In many newsrooms, children's issues are added to existing education or social service beats of already overworked reporters. Most news organizations don't think they cover the issues adequately, and many don't even try.

Some editors have considered starting a kidsbeat but shelved the idea because of slim resources; others just plainly aren't interested. The existence of a beat often depends on the serendipity of a motivated reporter with an interest in children's matters and a willing editor. Too many newspapers confine much of the substantial news about children and families to feature pages. Sadly, these assignments often still lack the prestige of political or business coverage.

And though the picture is slowly changing, children and teen-agers are too often portrayed by the media as troubled victims or crazed criminals. Much of the news about children and families is a one-shot crisis story about a child's abuse or death by violence, with little context or analysis of the deeper, systemic problems that put children and families in peril. Stories about crucial public policy issues get short shrift, leaving readers and viewers with little useful information about economic and societal forces driving up child abuse, tearing apart families and overwhelming child welfare and juvenile justice systems.

Detroit Free Press Executive Editor Heath J. Meriwether says his paper has developed "a real attention span" about children's issues: Kids aren't just "this year's hot subject but something enduring," he says.

But will the children's beat endure, or is it just the media's latest flavor of the month?

Reporting on children isn't a new phenomenon on journalism's time line, but the concept of an established beat devoted to children's issues is only a recent development. Journalists have been documenting the exploitation of children since the days of Joseph Pulitzer and his *New*

York World and reformer reporters like Nellie Bly in the 1880s through the muckraking era and beyond. In 1873, journalist Jacob Riis wrote about a 10-year-old girl found beaten and starved in New York, who was removed from her guardians through the intervention of the New York Society for the Prevention of Cruelty to Animals, a case which led to child welfare reforms and the creation of the New York Society for the Prevention of Cruelty to Children. In 1879, journalist Helen Campbell wrote a magazine series about the sufferings of women and children in New York slums, a body of work that she later expanded into a series of 21 articles in the *New York Tribune*. During the early 1900s, muckraker Edwin Markham wrote about the perilous working conditions of children in mills, coal mines and factories, and John Spargo chronicled the massive numbers of underfed school children in the country.

In the 1920s, Nellie Bly, a pioneer in investigative journalism best known for her daredevil, globe-circling stunts, turned her attention to the plight of children. Her stories on abandoned, abused and missing children often garnered front-page headlines in the *New York Evening Journal*. But she took it a step farther, becoming a crusading activist in her editorial-page columns for the adoption of the children of unwed mothers. "She found herself an instant clearinghouse for fractured families in distress," wrote Brooke Kroeger in her recent biography of Bly. Letters poured into Bly's column from indigent and unwed birth mothers seeking better homes for their children, and Bly became actively involved in arranging their adoptions. She once hosted a picnic trip for 750 orphans with donated cabs, buses, food and balloons. She even crusaded against mothers working outside the home except in extreme financial necessity, arguing in her column that "no children can be cared for and brought up and developed as they should where 'mother works downtown.'"

With the birth of television, the tradition continued in the 1960s through works like legendary CBS newsman Edward R. Murrow's "Harvest of Shame," which documented the plight of migrant workers and their children with poignant and horrific images of hungry children on grimy beds, gnawed by rats while their mother picked beans.

Through the 1960s and 1970s, individual journalists wrote about children's poverty, health and other issues, but it really wasn't until the 1980s that the concept of a beat focusing on children took root. Reporters like the *St. Louis Post-Dispatch*'s Martha Shirk, the *Denver Post*'s Carol Kreck, the *New York Times*' Carol Lawson, ABC News' Carole

Simpson and Rebecca Chase, and this writer, then at the *Wall Street Journal*, all launched children's beats in the 1980s.

A children's beat isn't the only way to cover children's issues, of course. Social service reporters are deeply involved with writing about the problems of children and families, while other journalists take a special interest in children's issues as they cover separate beats, most notably Alex Kotlowitz at the *Wall Street Journal*, whose front-page stories about the toll of violence on two brothers living in Chicago public housing inspired his award-winning book, *There Are No Children Here*. Social and political columnists like the *Washington Post*'s William Raspberry devote continuing attention to the web of problems confronting and connecting at-risk families. Still others have launched specialized family and parenting columns, and magazines ranging from the *New Yorker* to *Atlantic Monthly* to *Parenting, Parents Magazine* and *Child* began publishing serious journalism about children.

Though it spread roots in the 1980s, the beat didn't really flourish until the 1990s. Indeed, the Casey Journalism Center's survey of 62 newspapers and news services in 1993 showed that more than half had added children or family beats in the previous three years; in most newsrooms, the beats had been created in the previous 18 months. Since that survey was completed, at least another half-dozen newspapers have launched beats, teams or major projects to look at the lives of our children.

The pace of change is slower in the magazine and broadcast industries. The Casey Center survey showed a boom in magazines using children as their focus, though in a more limited way than newspapers. Although some broadcasters, too, are reacting to children and family stories with extra resources and airtime, commercial television and radio news is restrained by financial pressures, entertainment values, image and turf wars. Public radio and television, freed from depending on ratings, have spent more time on such issues.

Some of the noteworthy new models of reporting on children include front-page projects documenting children's problems for a year or more; full-time beats and teams covering issues of families, violence, and other social concerns; solutions-oriented journalism; and full-scale "crusades" where newspapers advocate for change and work for improvements. Examples include:

- Full-time beats and teams: *Newsday*'s "Society and Change" team covers religion, family issues and new social ideas, and the *Virginian Pilot* and

Ledger-Star of Norfolk share a five-reporter women/family/children team. During a time of tight budgets and little or no expansion in most of its other departments, the *San Jose Mercury News* created a full-time family-issues reporting position last year because of the topic's significance to its readers. New family beats have been created in recent years at the *New York Times, Washington Post, Cincinnati Enquirer, Portland Oregonian, Philadelphia Inquirer, Des Moines Register, Wichita Eagle* and many more.

- Solutions-oriented journalism: ABC World News Tonight's "American Agenda" and the *Chicago Tribune*'s "Killing Our Children" project are examples of journalism that tries to go beyond the problems to highlight model programs and suggest solutions.

- Long-term projects and crusades: Yearlong (or longer) projects and crusades by the *Detroit Free Press, Arizona Republic, Chicago Sun-Times* and *Chicago Tribune, Philadelphia Daily News* and the Bergen County, N.J., *Record* on child poverty, violence, abuse and juvenile justice have marshalled resources and guaranteed the issues space and front-page attention. Some of the papers run boxes with stories outlining ideas for ways people can help, and some try to be catalysts for change in their communities and state legislatures. The *Detroit Free Press* "Children First" crusade was kicked off in January 1993 with a prominent letter to readers from publisher Neal Shine announcing that the paper wanted to be "more than just a keeper of the statistics" by going farther than just reporting the problems to "making solutions happen." Beyond solid reporting on problems confronting children in Michigan, the paper's efforts include cultivating activism in the community, town hall meetings and raising money for children's initiatives.

Newspaper crusades have sparked controversy and raised the hackles of some journalists, who think they overstep traditional journalistic boundaries by abandoning objectivity. But there is a sense among others that these activist efforts are not only permissible but necessary and long overdue, as long as they are grounded in fairness, accuracy and aggressive reporting. "I call it a journalism that stands for something," says the *Free Press*'s Meriwether.

Children-oriented projects also tap into the "public journalism" notion of reconnecting with communities and becoming participants in public problem solving. "For all its strengths, the traditional definition of journalism is no longer adequate," warned James Batten, chairman and CEO of Knight-Ridder Inc., at an American Press Institute seminar on urban issues. "If we only report this crisis and that dilemma—no matter how brilliantly—we risk leaving already demoralized readers and communities feeling even more dispirited and hopeless."

Glenn Ritt, editor of *The Record* in Bergen County, N.J., which is involved in a mammoth project on juvenile justice and violence, says his paper is acting as "the glue of the community: the connector, the empowering institution that will listen and then not just lay the problem out there but get involved in helping to solve it." Hundreds of hours of hard-hitting reporting resulted in an ongoing series called "Delinquent Justice." The paper also held seminars in its office for county prosecutors, judges and lawmakers. "We are going to accept, as hard as it is for many of us, the premise that we could be partners with government, in particular," says Ritt.

But the debate continues. "The traditional role of journalism when done the best it can be done is still more than adequate," says Ann Marie Lipinski, the *Chicago Tribune*'s deputy managing editor. "I am a little nervous about doing the other."

The emergence of a children's beat is an important development because it professionalizes the reporting topic and puts it on a level playing field with more traditional beats, while also focusing the attention of sources in the community and focusing reporting within the media organization itself. Media organizations without a reporter assigned to children's issues often have to start each story from scratch, developing new sources as they go.

The beat can be defined in many ways. Some journalists focus on at-risk families, while others include the struggles of middle-class families, too. It has the potential to be one of the richest, meatiest beats around. "I think my job is the best job in network TV," says ABC's Rebecca Chase, who does stories about cutting-edge issues like welfare, teen pregnancy, juvenile delinquency, health care and child abuse. But the beat can be diminished by how it is defined, she warns. "You say 'family' and people think you're doing tea parties and kids—you know, Barney stories or something."

Why has the beat become so prominent after years of being on the back burner? Margaret Engel, a reporter on leave from the *Washington Post* who directs the Alicia Patterson Foundation, conducted the Casey Journalism Center's newspaper and magazine research. She found two motives cited repeatedly for this new interest: financial, as market surveys show newspapers must win back women readers; and civic, as editors mirror society in belatedly recognizing the national importance of a healthy, productive youth population. Kids in America are no longer seen but not heard.

Engel reports that demographics, combined with a belated recognition of reader interests, are pushing these emerging beats. The baby boomers are dictating national attention to whatever life phase they achieve. Baby boomers fill the newsrooms, and they have young children. Suddenly, topics like child custody, immunizations, day care, divorce and blended families have urgency and relevancy to newsroom decision-makers.

At the same time, national policy-makers are drawing attention to the declining well-being of American children and the underlying, connective tissue of problems, including teen pregnancy, child abuse and neglect, dropping education levels and rising violent crime among youths.

"These are social, economic and educational issues and they're definitely getting more attention than they did 10 years ago," says Lawrence Goodrich, features editor of the *Christian Science Monitor.*

The growth of newsroom reorganizations is also aiding nontraditional beats. The rise in interest in children and families represents dramatic change in newsrooms and new definitions about front-page news. Many editors find it is directly related to the crumbling of traditional newsroom norms, as reporters break away from covering buildings and boards to writing about individuals and groups. Nearly half the newspapers surveyed by the Casey Center have set up beats that break down old fiefdoms. Typical is the Columbia, S.C., State, with its "circle" teams reporting on quality of life (environment, food, housing, crime and health) and passages (relationships, learning and geriatric issues).

The interest in children and family topics has been helped by several benchmarks, cited repeatedly in our research with editors and reporters across the country. First lady Hillary Rodham Clinton's interest in children's rights and protections has elevated these subjects, as did Bill Clinton's presidential campaign, which made children's policy issues a priority. The commitment by Attorney General Janet Reno to children's issues has also played a role.

Other benchmarks include the movement of male journalists into these areas, helping ease the "girl ghetto" fears of some reporters. Prominent front-page projects by the *Detroit Free Press, Chicago Tribune, Chicago Sun-Times* and other publications have put A-list reporters on children's issues. The Arizona Republic, which began a yearlong crusade last year called "Saving Arizona's Children," has used its best reporters and generous amounts of front-page space. Another important benchmark was the exhaustive front-page 10-part series, "Children of the Shadows," last year in the *New York Times*, a newspaper with the power and prestige to set the agenda for other publications.

If journalism awards are any indication of what journalism values, then children's issues have certainly arrived. Stories, editorials and commentary about children dominated journalism's most vaunted awards this year, with Pulitzers awarded to one of the stories in the *Times*' "Shadows" series, William Raspberry's commentaries, and *Chicago Tribune* editorials and science writing about children; the *Tribune*'s "Killing Our Children" series won the Robert F. Kennedy Journalism Award's Grand Prize, and *Philadelphia Inquirer* reporter John Woestendiek's work on homeless families won the Ernie Pyle Award.

Symbolic, too, is the launching of the Casey Journalism Center for Children and Families last year to serve as a national resource for journalists covering issues about disadvantaged children and families and the institutions that serve them. The Center, part of the University of Maryland College of Journalism, is funded by the Annie E. Casey Foundation of Baltimore, the nation's largest philanthropy devoted to disadvantaged children. Further evidence of the rising interest in the beat was the National Conference on Children and the News Media at Stanford University earlier this year, which brought together many key journalists and children's advocates to examine the news media's impact on children. And the Columbia University Graduate School of Journalism, which hosted the landmark 1992 conference "Focus on Children: The Beat of the Future," is launching a new children's journalism fellowship program in 1995.

The children's beat isn't very old, but it's already having growing pains. Journalists wrestle daily with vexing issues. Should the media be advocates for children, and if so, how far should they go? Should journalists use children's names when reporting stories? How far should they go to protect children who aren't savvy about the press? How should they handle sensitive information told to them by children that could cause problems for the family?

One of the most urgent issues is how the media can better convey depth and detail about the causes and consequences of children's problems. Public policy and solutions to problems like juvenile violence and teen pregnancy evolve in slow, complicated ways, and the media often have no patience for stories that can't be summarized in a "sound bite" or a "nut graph."

Deadline constraints, shrinking news holes and increasing pressures from tabloid-style television and newspapers to highlight the sensational aspects of stories all play a role. Racial and ethnic stereotypes in media coverage of youth and crime also create a distorted picture. Critics have charged that African American and Latino people are overwhelmingly portrayed as troubled on television news and that the *New York Times* "Shadows" series and similar newspaper projects focus almost exclusively on children of color. Other media projects have been criticized for bludgeoning readers with numbing news about at-risk children or creating pressure for misguided public policy solutions. In Chicago, the *Tribune*'s "Killing Our Children" series documented the death from homicide of every child under age 15 in the Chicago area in 1993 by displaying the body count in bold black numbers on the newspaper's front page with an accompanying story on the child's life. But not all children's advocates approve of such coverage—Chicago's Youth Communication director, Susan Herr, for example, calls it "paternal journalism" that covers kids without giving them their own voice.

Amidst these concerns, public cynicism about the press is soaring while polls show the public has scant understanding of the factors that contribute to the headlines on violence, teen pregnancy and child abuse.

"This is a generation that has so much to tell us," says Sandy Close, editor of Pacific News Service, a weekly op-ed service in San Francisco. "Yet the media treat it like a world of pathology, a sense of fatalism, as if these kids are doomed."

Scherrie Goettsch, features editor of the Columbia, Mo., *Daily Tribune,* notes, "It's sad but true, but there has to be a multiple murder to get front-page attention for most children's issues."

A study commissioned by Children Now, the children's advocacy group that co-hosted a National Conference on Children and the News Media, showed that nearly half of news stories about children depict them as victims or perpetrators of crime, while fewer than 4 percent examined their economic woes. "With 14 million American children living in poverty, even a rookie reporter can see that the media is missing the real story. The reason is simple: Violence sells," concludes the group's conference report.

In fact, 48 percent of all television stories and 40 percent of all newspaper stories about kids concern crime, according to the Children Now analysis; at a time when national crime rates remained the same, only one story in three had anything to do with policy.

In their defense, journalists point out the constant tension between daily demands and the need for longer-range thinking. "The big-picture stories, the in-depth series—they are all luxuries to us," says Leslie Baldacci, who launched the *Chicago Sun-Times*' families beat several years ago before moving to the editorial staff. Shrinking resources and leaner staffs limit time and coverage. "We do not have a single reporter in our city who exclusively covers juvenile court, and I bet that is true in most of your cities, too."

Journalists also say news organizations must not try to protect readers and viewers from the hard truth about the peril to children's lives, even though some readers may be shocked and horrified.

The *Chicago Tribune*'s Lipinski says she clung to a letter from a suburban reader during her paper's child homicide project. It read: "I'm tired of picking up my newspaper every day and reading about these kids; it has really gotten to be too much. I have three words of advice to you: Keep it up."

Cathy Trost is director of the Casey Journalism Center for Children and Families, a University of Maryland resource center for journalists covering issues about disadvantaged children and families. She is a former Wall Street Journal *reporter who covered children's and family issues.*

8

How the News Media "See" Kids

Dale Kunkel

America's future is in the hands of its children. Children come in all shapes and sizes, many colors, and a wide range of conditions, from secure and sustained to homeless and hungry. Like most concerns important to our country, the subject of children is covered by the news media, which fulfill an essential role in informing the population about the issues facing today's youth. By serving as gatekeepers of the messages the public receives about the condition of children in American society, the press plays a pivotal role in influencing awareness of child-related issues. Perhaps more importantly, the information conveyed by the media ultimately serves as the foundation for public opinion about the need for policy action to promote children's interests on a wide range of issues.

How well do the news media do their job of covering children and child policy issues? How extensive is the coverage of this important topic, and what shape and form does it take? Most simply, what picture of children does the nation's press paint for the public? Surprisingly, this topic has largely escaped the focus of media researchers. This study addresses these questions through a systematic analysis of national news content devoted to children and child-related topics.

In order to get a representative look at how U.S. media cover children, the study assessed the news content delivered daily for the entire month of November 1993 in five major U.S. metropolitan newspapers (*Atlanta Constitution, Chicago Tribune, Houston Chronicle, Los Angeles Times, New York Times*), and on the nightly newscasts of the three major commercial television networks (ABC, CBS and NBC). Thus, the conclusions of this report are based on a significant sample of news coverage collected from eight of the nation's most important news sources.

The study yielded a total of 949 stories, most (840) appearing in the newspaper sample, understandable given the inequities inherent in the "space" available to newspapers compared to network television. Both print and TV news can at least lay claim to regular treatment of child topics, however. The newspapers surveyed published an average of 4.6 news stories involving children per edition, while even the television networks delivered an average of 1.3 stories per newscast.

A predictable distinction between print and television coverage was the finding that whereas 18 percent (150) of all newspaper "stories" were opinion-based (e.g., columns, editorials), not a single TV segment was devoted to commentary or editorializing. This, of course, reflects the prevailing pattern in television news, which has seen most commentaries fall by the wayside.

Roughly half (49 percent) of the child-related stories included in the newspapers appeared in the front section, with 11 percent of all print stories about kids making it onto the front page. The *Chicago Tribune,* which has established a commitment to emphasize child coverage, particularly in the area of crime and violence, was the clear leader in this regard, with a total of 32 front-page stories on children during the month, or an average of more than one per day.

An interesting finding emerged in the assessment of story length. For newspapers, nearly three-quarters of all stories contained fewer than 1,000 words, which is roughly the equivalent of four double-spaced typewritten pages, or approximately 20 column inches. Considering that stories shorter than three column inches (roughly 150 words) in length were excluded from the study, this finding underscores the brevity of most print coverage regarding children.

While the average newspaper story ran a total of only 850 words—or about 17 column inches—substantial space was devoted to a handful of unusual stories. For example, the single longest piece, which ran more than 9,000 words, was a *Los Angeles Times* analysis of a case of conjoined twins who shared a single heart and their parents' battle to convince surgeons to try to save one of them.

Television stories ranged from 10 seconds to just over five minutes in length, the amount of time devoted to an ABC "American Agenda" story about how young children deal with a grandparent who suffers from Alzheimer's disease. The mean length for all children's stories on television was calculated at exactly two minutes.

Stories were categorized according to topic, with six general areas emerging from the analysis: crime/violence, education, family, health, cultural issues and economics. By a substantial margin, the most predominant type of news story about children involved reports of crime and violence. Such coverage accounted for 48 percent of all television news stories and 40 percent of all news reports in the newspapers.

The largest share of the coverage of crime and violence was devoted to "breaking news" accounts of crimes either committed by or against children (12 percent of all stories for both newspapers and television), followed closely by stories regarding the investigation and prosecution of such crimes (10 percent of all newspaper stories, 8 percent of all television stories). The coverage of sex crimes against children was also extensive, with crimes involving child molestation and child pornography accounting for 10 percent of all the child-related stories on television, and for 5 percent of the stories in newspapers.

While one might wonder if these findings were influenced strongly by extensive media coverage of any unusual stories, this does not seem to have been the case. For example, perhaps the most prominent child-related story to emerge during the study period was the allegation that singer Michael Jackson was a child molester. This incident, however, accounted for no more than 9.6 percent of all child-related stories involving crime and violence on television, and for only 3.7 percent of all such stories in the newspaper. (Not all coverage of the Michael Jackson story fell within the parameters of this study, which examined only stories reflecting a primary emphasis on child-related issues. Many stories on this subject essentially omitted any treatment of the actual issue of child molestation [for example, reporting on Jackson's likely whereabouts] and thus were not coded.)

Although crime and violence clearly dominated the overall news media coverage of children, there was also substantial treatment of stories about education, with newspapers (25 percent of all stories) exceeding television (15 percent of all stories) in their attention to this topic. It is clear where most media attention regarding children falls—in both newspapers and television, nearly two-thirds of the child-related coverage fell in the categories crime/violence or education. The remaining one-third of the coverage was split nearly equally among three major topic areas: the family, cultural issues and health. The most neglected of all major topics—economic concerns—was featured in only 4 percent of all stories involving children. Falling within this realm were such issues as child poverty, homelessness and child welfare, as well as child care and family leave policy. Across these four major topic areas (family, cultural issues, health, economics), almost no differences existed between the proportions of coverage found in newspapers and on television.

Each story examined was evaluated on a number of dimensions reflecting the nature of its coverage of the topic. These findings indicate that there is a high degree of consistency in the approaches employed for reporting the news in newspapers and television. Both rely extensively on expert sources (87 percent for newspapers; 76 percent for television), both report statistical information and present some historical context in nearly half of their stories, and both tend to incorporate information from parents or children themselves in only about one in four stories.

The study also evaluated the extent to which the news media focused on topics of particular concern, such as minority group issues or gender-related differences. On these issues as well as the subject of developmental differences across children of different ages, there was little coverage at all, with only a handful of stories in either medium devoted primarily to such topics.

Only about one-third of the stories in either medium devoted any attention to public policy concerns, and only about one-quarter of all stories featured a primary focus on policy issues. Of those stories that did address child-related policy concerns, 87 percent included specific factual information about current policy. Newspaper stories seemed to assume a somewhat more negative tone, as reflected in the finding that newspapers were more likely to identify problems with existing policy than was television (68 percent of policy stories for newspapers vs. 53 percent for television) and also less likely to identify any successes accomplished by current policies (28 percent of policy stories for newspapers vs. 37 percent for television).

Stories with a primary focus on policy most frequently addressed the topics of education (11 percent of all stories) or crime and violence (5 percent of all stories). Beyond these two topics, however, there was relatively scant coverage of policy concerns in such areas as child health, family functioning or economic concerns; none of these topics accounted for more than 2 percent of all child-related news stories.

The news media surveyed seem to provide a substantial number of stories addressing child-related topics. With more space to fill, newspapers naturally are more thorough in this regard, offering an average of 4.6 stories per issue, although even television devoted more than one story per edition of the network news. Many would assume that newspapers tend to convey a greater amount of information per story than television, yet the findings of this study suggest that question may warrant closer examination. With the average television story running a full two minutes and the comparable mean for newspaper story length observed to be only 850 words, there may not be as great a disparity between the two media as one might expect.

Perhaps the most compelling finding is that the news media's dominant frame for child coverage involves crime and violence. For television, such coverage accounted for nearly half (48 percent) of all stories about children, 40 percent for newspapers. In contrast, the news media provided less overall coverage for all other public policy issues combined than was allocated to reports of crime and violence; both newspapers and television devoted only 35 percent of their stories to any policy-related content. An even smaller proportion of stories reflected a *primary* focus on policy.

Of the policy topics addressed by the news media, education received the most attention, followed by crime and violence policy concerns. Almost entirely overlooked were many important public policy issues that fall in the areas of family, health and economic concerns; each of these three areas accounted for no more than 2 percent of the overall news coverage.

While there may be substantial *quantity* of coverage of children, it would be difficult to characterize that coverage as balanced. The emphasis placed on reports of crime, with children portrayed as both victims and perpetrators of violence, seems to skew the information the press provides to the public, which may in turn diminish the public's perception of the relative importance of other child-related concerns. While it is impossible to know for sure, at least from the present data, it may be that the extensive coverage devoted to crime and violence serves to displace other child-oriented coverage.

In order for the public to gain the information it needs to weigh the important public policy issues facing America's children, it is essential for the news media to cover the entire range of concerns that impact children's future. There is no doubt that crime and violence is a serious issue facing America's youth. Yet without discounting the seriousness of that issue, this research underscores the need for greater breadth and balance in the news media's coverage of child-related issues in order to effectively inform the public on all the important issues relating to children in American society.

Dale Kunkel is associate professor of communication at the University of California-Santa Barbara. This essay grows from his research for the Los Angeles-based child advocacy group Children Now.

9

Children Like Me—Where Do We Fit In?

María Elena Gutiérrez

Mary sits at the snack table waiting for the other children to join her. She sees Donald coming toward her and says, "I'm peach and you're brown." Donald looks at her. "I'm black," he says. Both children smile and Donald sits by Mary.

A teacher overhearing this exchange calmly observes, "Mary and Donald, you are both right. Donald's skin color is brown, but he and his family call themselves 'black' or 'African American.'" The classmates start comparing their hand color, hair color, eye color. Tommy says he is "white." The teacher gets a sheet of white paper and asks Tommy, "Are you this color?" Tommy reflects. "No." The children decide Tommy is pink.

A group of children stands around a water table, washing dolls they've played with during the day. Ray washes a doll that he says "has dirt on it"; once the sand is rinsed off, Ray discovers the doll isn't dirty anymore. Amy, who is helping clean up, says, "Ray, my doll is clean too, but she is brown."

Both dolls are clean, the teacher explains, but the brown doll's color won't wash off. The teacher, Mexican American, is dark-skinned. She washes her hands and holds them up for the children. "My brown color won't wash off either." Ray touches his teacher's hands and says matter of factly, "You're not dirty. Your hands are just brown."

Brian stares at Harry's hair, and decides to touch it. Harry pushes Brian's hand away. A teacher steps in and Brian asks permission to touch Harry's hair. It feels funny, Brian concludes, puzzled. The teacher explains that Harry's hair has a different texture than Brian's hair.

These are real-life examples from my former school yard that show how 2-year-olds can learn about themselves and their differences. It is an atmosphere in which asking is OK, and what they are asking and wanting to understand is validated and discussed. The teachers in this program are trained to listen to the questions: Questions children ask are important.

Even at this early age, children try to make sense out of their world. Research and the experiences of teachers show that children can be preprejudiced by the age of 2 to 2 1/2; by 5 they know most racial stereotypes. How can this be? How can they pick up these attitudes at such a young age? The answer is found in the world around them, especially in what they experience in their homes and through the media.

By the time they are 5, children are well attuned to ways of hurting one another. Differences—and the way they are interpreted—often cause problems. Examples:

- Tina won't play with Sandra because she has "slit eyes."
- Norman says Manuel is a "dirty Mexican."
- Naomi makes fun of any child who speaks any language other than English: They are all foreigners, she parrots, who should go back where they came from.

Except for the family, the media have perhaps the most powerful impact on children's attitudes toward the world and others in it. For the most part, the images they hear and see on television and elsewhere in the electronic age are violent and negative, and parents often are in a quandary about why their children have so stereotyped other groups. As a teacher I hear parents protest, helplessly and defensively, "They didn't learn it at home." My response is always, "What are they watching and listening to on TV? 'Sesame Street'? The news? 'Beavis and Butt-Head'? 'Power Rangers'?"

They shrug. Too often, parents don't pay much attention to what their children watch on television, what they overhear in adult conversations, who their children are exposed to and what type of books and magazines they read. Unless they do, how can parents explain to their children that what they see and hear in the media and elsewhere is skewed, stereotyped, incorrect?

For their part, the media seem either unaware or uncaring that they still tend to present a white worldview to audiences that increasingly

are racially diverse. This diversity is both more pronounced and potentially more accepted at younger ages than in the adult population. By
the second half of the next century, when today's preschoolers move
past middle age, the majority of the U.S. population will be not white,
but of Asian, African, Latino or Native American descent. By 2000, just
five years away, California will be the first state where minorities will
be the majority, demographers predict.

American television's perception of what is beautiful, desirable, "cool"
is not where the U.S. population is heading. But we and our children
still learn from the images television projects, lessons that conform less
and less to the world around us. If American children are to learn how
they will fit into the increasingly multicultural society that is coming,
the people who create television's images of America need to start reflecting our nation and our people as we are. If we and our children are
to get along with one another, we, like the toddlers in my school yard,
first must learn to become more comfortable with our differences.

As a Chicana child growing up in the East Los Angeles Mexican
American barrio, my earliest and strongest memories of Anglos and
other groups came from my exposure to them through television. Programs like "Leave it to Beaver," "Ozzie and Harriet," "Amos 'n' Andy,"
"Beulah," "Hopalong Cassidy" and "The Cisco Kid" all showed me a
world very different from mine, both in lifestyle and in portrayal of
Latinos and Anglos.

Where, I wondered, was someone on TV who looked like me? Where
were my family and friends? When I did see someone who looked like
me, they were disappointing stereotypes whose exaggerated Latin tem-
perament and accents were the focus of jokes, setting the stage for ridicule—Carmen Miranda, Ricky Ricardo, Pancho on "The Cisco Kid"
and Pepino on "The Real McCoys." Other characters—the heroic
"Zorro," Don Diego de la Vega and the "Cisco Kid" himself—were more
positive, but also distinctly Spanish, not Mexican like me and those
around me. Opposite these heroic, light-skinned Europeans played overweight Mexican buffoons—Sergeant García on "Zorro" and Pancho on
"The Cisco Kid." And, as in U.S. television today, Latinas never appeared on my childhood television, except for the few fat, happy mama-
citas, sexy señoritas or Latin spitfires.

My favorite time in elementary school was when the teacher read us
books (even if she read in English and most of us spoke Spanish as our

first language). But who were Cinderella and Snow White to me? I liked them, but they didn't look like the folks I knew. By the end of kindergarten I had learned that who I was and what my family valued—even our language—was neither valued nor even reflected at my school or on television. It was not until I was in college that I began to realize that who I was and what I valued were important.

A few years ago I consulted on developmental issues and children with Disney studios, which was contemplating a program for preschoolers. I found myself frustrated by animators whose whole perspective was channeled through stereotypes. We had long conversations; they explained that they use stereotypes because they tell a story in a quick picture. It was very difficult to get them to acknowledge that these "little pictures" that they found so useful were doing a lot of damage to the people who were portrayed and the audiences that viewed them.

From the perspective of children and adults who are not Anglo, media images in the 1990s are not much better than when I was growing up. At my center in Alameda, there are children who are Chinese, Vietnamese, Korean, Pakistani, Erithian, Latino and African American. Where are they and their families and friends on television today? What do these American children think and feel, not seeing themselves on afternoon TV?

María Elena Gutiérrez is supervisor of the Woodstock Child Development Center in the Alameda Unified School District in Alameda, Calif.

III

The Child Audience

10

Symposium III

Jana Eisenberg

Leading off Part III, which examines children as audience, we turn to five contributors, who know their audiences well, for a shorthand primer on issues concerning the consumers of media's messages. These five experts include an all-time all-star of children's television, a congresswoman who has worked long and hard in this area, two scholars, and an editor of a kids' sports magazine.

Fred Rogers, host and creator, "Mister Rogers' Neighborhood." Excerpted from the PBS supplement to the New Yorker *(Nov. 30, 1992):*

Television may be the only electrical appliance that's more useful after it's turned off. One of our favorite stories here in this Neighborhood is about a 2-year-old who, after watching our visit with Yo-Yo Ma, started using a chopstick for a bow on an old guitar. His mother wrote us: "I've never seen anything like it. He cried until I told him we'd try to find some way for him to 'play the cello.'" That was three years ago, and recently we learned that that little boy is still playing the cello, and his mother has decided to learn, too.

Television isn't something that's just *watched*. It's swallowed...and sometimes digested. We in public television have a responsibility to ensure that what we present to children is as healthy for them as the food they need to survive.

The "educational" part of television, which is at the foundation of PBS, is primarily producers learning all we can about the needs and feelings of children and their families. For us, the question is not, "What can we *sell* them?"...or even, "What can we *give* them?"...but rather, "Who are *they*?" and "What do *they* bring to the television set?"

Television is seen by children as something that their parents provide. In a young child's mind, then, parents condone what's on the television set, just like they choose what's in the refrigerator or on the stove. That's why we must be especially careful with what we produce, with the people we present and with the attitudes we show in television relationships—attitudes of respect, kindness, healthy curiosity, determination and love...just as parents would want for their children.

Todd Gitlin, author and professor of sociology, University of California-Berkeley:

There is far too much TV enticing children. Understandably, the prime interest of programmers is to seduce children to watch more of it. That's a social problem, one with no ready solution. But, clearly, the commercialism of children's TV is detrimental to developing a sensibility adequate to the modern world. The interest in programming for children periodically displayed by network executives is a cynical business to deflect regulators.

There is a glut of entertaining noise and pictures, which have deleterious effects on children. This inclines them to look for entertainment in everything they do or see, but this is resistible.

There is clearly good stuff on TV for children—by way of nature shows and didactic lessons. There are probably not enough of these outside of cable, and 35 percent to 40 percent of American households—mostly poor—don't even have cable. American children deserve access to the educational programming that I see when I am abroad, such as language lessons. But there are also a great many programs on prime time and elsewhere that are harmful—partly because they're violent and partly because they're stupid, speedy and brainless.

TV violence is a minor cause of actual negative effects. The velocity, gaudiness and high-dose stimulus that kids get from TV and the nonstop bombardment with messages equating the good life to consumer splendor are more destructive. The gaudiness of the view of the world presented by TV is itself a factor leading toward restless dissatisfaction that translates into criminality.

Rep. Patricia Schroeder, D-Colo., head of the House Committee on Children, Youth and Families:

Kids are seen by media as little consumers. It's as if they are saying to kids, "Our nation depends upon YOU! You must consume." Very few things in media do anything other than entertain or terrorize children. Television could be a very positive tool, but it seems like everybody got together and decided to bring it down to the lowest common denominator. I find that sad.

Cable can be better. Nickelodeon has done good things on the environment and, in conjunction with Linda Ellerbee's production company, Lucky Duck, good things on AIDS and has presented forums where kids can relate to other young people.

I saw evidence that kids respond to interactive media at the beginning of this congressional session. The Congress had never had an opening party that included families, and Nickelodeon came and put one on. They set up a corner with a video camera and said to the children, "If you have a message for the new administration, just stand there, push the button and give it." And to watch these kids seriously think about what they wanted to say was wonderful. They had no qualms about doing it.

I find all that part good. But the public doesn't see that. I see it as a legislator every day. School groups win national prizes for debates on all kinds of important issues, but they just can't get the coverage back home. If they came in here and shot someone, they'd be on the front page.

Craig Neff, managing editor, Sports Illustrated for Kids:

Finally, the media recognize children as an audience for something more than cartoons. Kids can now choose from 200 magazines published just for them. They can watch news for kids on TV and read special children's pages in many major newspapers.

But are the media doing a better job of enlightening adults about the problems that children face? Are they giving kids a voice that the leaders of our society can hear? I think not. The media fail at both ends of the news spectrum. They give paltry coverage to the wonderful achievements of kids and do an inadequate job of placing adult readers and viewers into the shoes of children who are losing their future to gangs, crime, teen pregnancy and other social plagues. Basically, they don't talk to kids enough.

With their candid observations and strong sense of right and wrong, kids can enlighten us. They can clarify our vision and our priorities. But kids still feel powerless and voiceless, and the media aren't doing much to change that.

Jane D. Brown, journalism professor, University of North Carolina-Chapel Hill:

Only one in 25 sexual messages on prime-time TV suggests that sexual behavior may have negative consequences. Unmarried people on television have sex four to eight times more frequently than married people. The media have become important sex educators for our youth. Teens seek sexual information from the media as they create a sense of themselves as sexual human beings. Unfortunately, girls learn from media portrayals that they will not succeed unless they are beautiful and popular with men. Boys learn that they can expect to have sex with women without an enduring relationship.

The media should present more responsible portrayals of sexuality. Yes, sex can be fun and pleasurable, but early, unprotected and unloving sex is potentially dangerous. Our youth need to know that there is more to life. Wouldn't it be great to see and read more about girls thinking about careers or friendships with other girls; boys seeking love and commitment; youth involved in political issues?

11

By the Numbers—What Kids Watch

Larry McGill

Amidst all the concern in recent years about children's exposure to potentially harmful television programming, there has been surprisingly little attention paid (outside of the TV industry itself) to what children actually watch.

The assumption is that the bulk of what children see on television is accounted for by Saturday morning kids' programming on the networks, with PBS and Nickelodeon programming rounding out the rest of the picture. While kids do flock to those sources, data suggest they represent less than half of what kids actually spend their time watching.

First of all, how much time do kids spend in front of the TV? Less than you might think. Contrary to the stereotypical view that kids spend all their time glued to the tube, they actually spend far less time watching television than do most adults. Nielsen data from the 1992-93 television season indicate that children ages 2 to 11 spent an average of about 22 hours watching television per week, or a little over three hours per day. In contrast, men 18 and over spent an average of almost 28.5 hours per week watching television—more than four hours per day—and women 18 and over, the heaviest users of television, spent nearly 50 percent more time watching television than children 2 to 11, an average of 32.75 hours of television per week, or 4 hours, 40 minutes per day. If parents are truly concerned about how much television their children are watching, they would do well to look first at their own performance as role models.

Further, even with the explosion of cable programming options, children watch significantly less television now than just a decade ago. As recently as the 1984–85 television season, children 2 to 11 were watching as much as 26.75 hours of television per week. In 1992–93, kids' viewing was 18 percent lower.

But this does not necessarily mean that children are spending less time in front of the TV set. Although comparative data for prior years are not available, figures from February 1994 indicate significant levels of VCR usage and video-game playing by children 2 to 11. At any given moment (averaged across the entire week on a 24-hour-a-day basis) roughly 3 percent of *all* children 2 to 11 are either using a VCR or playing a video game on their home television set. This exceeds the average 24-hour-a-day ratings among these kids for *any* single source of television programming. Put another way, if watching videos and playing video games were a network, it would be the No. 1 network on television among kids 2 to 11. These activities peak on weekend afternoons, when 7.2 percent of all American kids watch videos or play video games on Saturdays, and 6.3 percent on Sundays.

So when do kids watch television? If you answered Saturday morning, you wouldn't be wrong, but just as many kids watch every weekday late afternoon and early evening and during Monday to Sunday prime time. During each of these time periods, roughly 10 million children ages 2 to 11—about 28 percent of all kids—are watching television at any given moment. Kids' viewing actually peaks between 7:30 and 8 p.m. weekdays; when nearly *33 percent* of all children 2 to 11 are watching television.

As a proportion of the total audience, however, the Saturday morning time period provides the greatest concentration of children. Slightly more than a quarter of the total Saturday-morning viewing audience (26 percent) is children, compared to 15 percent of the Monday-Friday late afternoon/early evening audience and just 10 percent of the prime-time audience. But even though kids make up a smaller proportion of the *total* TV audience in these latter two time periods, the fact remains that just as many kids are watching at these times as are watching on Saturday mornings.

In other words, just as many kids are being exposed to prime-time and late afternoon/early evening programming as Saturday morning programming. In fact, since the total number of prime-time hours (22) and late afternoon/early evening hours (15) during the week is significantly greater than the number of hours on a Saturday morning (7 a.m.

to 1 p.m.), children are exposed to substantially more programming airing at those times than they are to Saturday morning programming.

What do kids watch in greatest numbers? During the 1993–94 season, the 10 highest-rated programs among children 2 to 11 were all sitcoms airing during prime time on two of the four major broadcast networks (eight on ABC and two on Fox). The most-watched shows among children 2 to 11 were ABC's "Home Improvement," "Step by Step" and "Full House," each with an average rating of 13.5 in that age group. The highest-rated Saturday morning program ("Mighty Morphin Power Rangers") ranked 19th on the list, while the highest-rated syndicated program ("Family Matters," a sitcom originally on ABC) ranked 35th. Although exact data for cable programs were not available, it's clear that the highest-rated cable program would not make the top 100 most-watched shows among kids.

PBS ratings are not available on a national basis, so direct comparisons with the ratings noted above are not strictly possible. But PBS ratings in selected cities are suggestive: A review of the ratings in New York and Boston in May 1994, for example, indicates that if national ratings were available, several PBS programs might rank among the top 50 most-watched shows by children 2 to 11. In fact "Barney," PBS's No. 1 show among kids, could conceivably rank among the nation's top 20 most-watched kidshows.

Of course, kids 2 to 11 are by no means a homogeneous group. Preschoolers' viewing habits are significantly different from those of children 6 to 11; not only do they prefer to watch different programs, but they are also available during dayparts when 6- to 11-year-olds are at school, and they also tend to be heavier users of videotapes. PBS's "Barney" is easily the most-watched program among 2- to 5-year-olds (with ratings perhaps as much or more than 50 percent higher than any other show on television), while two other PBS offerings—"Shining Time Station" and "Lamb Chop's Play-Along"—would probably also place among the top 10.

So despite well-publicized (and legitimate) concerns about young children being victimized by violent cartoons—"Ninja Turtles" and assorted other superheroes—and cynical, product-based offerings such as "He-Man" and "My Little Pony," ratings numbers indicate that kids' attention is turned elsewhere. What's on does not necessarily equal what kids watch.

Larry McGill is the Center's director of research and administration. He is grateful for the assistance of Horst Stipp, director of social and development research at NBC, in preparing this essay.

12

Six Myths About Television and Children

Milton Chen

A curious mythology has grown up around television and its effects on children. Together, these myths would have us believe that TV is single-handedly turning kids into couch potatoes, frying their brains, shortening their attention spans and lowering their academic abilities. Supposedly, TV is a dark and foreboding menace in our children's lives. These myths can be traced to the simplistic, yet persistent, view that TV, as a medium, has effects of its own that transcend any specific content.

Since teachers, parents and the media themselves constantly propagate these myths, it is important to examine them. Although some children who watch TV 30 or 40 hours a week struggle in school, there are deeper reasons why they do besides time spent watching television. Are their parents taking an active role in helping their children learn? Or are these latchkey children who are left to their own devices? Television's effects do depend on how much we watch and, more importantly, on *what* we watch.

None of the following myths is supported by substantive research. In fact, research has often contradicted them. Unfortunately, the propagators of these myths have done a much better job of marketing their opinions than the researchers who have done the studies to debunk them. So here I present, in point-counterpoint fashion, six pervasive myths about TV.

Myth no. 1: TV is a passive medium. My child will become a listless couch potato.
Fact no. 1: Educational TV shows can actively engage your child, physically and intellectually. The activity can and should continue after the show is over.

There are at least two kinds of passivity: physical and intellectual. One of the most common myths about TV viewing is that it is, by definition, a passive activity. Contrary to popular belief, neither physical nor intellectual passivity is an immutable fact of TV viewing, especially for children.

As any parent of a child who watches "Barney & Friends" or "Sesame Street" knows, young viewers are physically engaged, singing, clapping and stretching along with their favorite characters, especially when the shows invite them to do so. Programs such as these also encourage intellectual activity as children learn important concepts, from counting to kindness.

One overlooked and underused feature of television is its ability to prompt viewers to read aloud. Some current children's shows, such as "Ghostwriter" and "Beakman's World," use animation and graphics to highlight key words for viewers to read and pronounce as they are watching.

Many other examples of children's TV demonstrate how young viewers can exercise their cognitive muscles while they watch. A U.S. Department of Education study found that "contrary to popular assertions, children are cognitively active during television viewing in an attempt to form a coherent, connected understanding of television programs."

This activity shouldn't cease after the show is over. The best children's programs provide activities and tips for teachers, child-care providers and parents on related follow-up activities. Whether it's folding origami with Shari Lewis of "Lamb Chop's Play-Along," writing a letter to "Ghostwriter" or borrowing a "Reading Rainbow" book from the library, television can be a creative source of active learning rather than the presumed death of it.

Myth no. 2: TV stunts the healthy growth of the brain. It zaps a child's brain waves.
Fact no. 2: Brain-wave patterns during TV viewing are very similar to brain activity during other activities.

Some educators and commentators, like educational psychologist Dr. Jane Healy, have suggested that TV viewing has a deleterious effect on brain development, that because it is a visual medium, it may overstimulate the right hemisphere (responsible for visual processing) and understimulate the left hemisphere (responsible for language and processing of print). The critique often invokes technical language about "frontal-lobe development," "neural pathways" and "alpha and beta waves," creating both confusion and concern in the minds of many parents.

Does television really interfere with children's brain functioning and zap their synapses? It can seem plausible, especially when such claims are made in jargon with the appearance of medical authority.

A neuropsychologist's authoritative review should put these fears to rest. Dr. Katharine Fite of the Neuroscience and Behavior Program at the University of Massachusetts, Amherst, concluded: "In recent years, a number of claims have appeared in the popular media and press suggesting that television viewing has potentially detrimental effects on human brain development and/or brain activity. An extensive review of the published scientific literature provides no evidence to substantiate such beliefs."

Fite described two major findings from experiments that measured small electrical signals from the scalp, indicating brain activity. These studies found that during TV watching, viewers' brain-wave patterns are "quite similar to those that occur during other waking-state activities. Thus TV viewing should not be characterized as producing a passive or inattentive activity in the brain." She also reported that television is not, as argued, exclusively a right-brain activity.

Parents should rest easier, knowing this alarm about our children's gray matter is only a red herring. Instead, we should devote our own brain waves to the more important questions of what and how much our children are watching.

Myth no. 3: TV shortens a child's attention span.
Fact no. 3: Educational TV shows can actually increase a child's attention and cognitive skills.

Myth no. 3 and its close cousin, Myth no. 2, have been propagated by a small but prolific group of writers and educators who often turn their attack on one specific program. The object of their reproach? Not "Teenage Mutant Ninja Turtles" or the "Mighty Morphin Power Rangers." No, none other than "Sesame Street." The critique is an academic hit-and-run, since these individuals do not stop to conduct any research of their own, nor do they cite the wealth of research that has already been done on the program.

"Sesame Street" is the most widely researched television program in history. In fact, a bibliography published by Children's Television Workshop (CTW) in 1989 lists an astonishing 633 studies on its cognitive and social effects.

Yet some academics and writers insist that "Sesame Street" is a hazard to children's development. As Dr. Daniel Anderson, professor of psychology at the University of Massachusetts, Amherst, explains, these critics believe that the "rapid transitions between scenes... mesmerize children and interfere with their reflection and inference, so that the child is left only with memories of a jumbled, disconnected set of visual images."

But Anderson, who has studied the effect of "Sesame Street" on children's attention spans more thoroughly than anyone else, believes these critics do not give young children enough credit for their purposeful cognitive skills. He summarizes the findings: "The new research showed that the critique was wrong. The child viewer of 'Sesame Street,' rather than being a mesmerized zombie, is selective and intellectually active.... We have evidence that 'Sesame Street' actually enhances attentional and perceptual abilities.... Research on 'Sesame Street' has shown us that young children are far more capable than we previously believed."

Then why is "Sesame Street" so often the target of misguided and uninformed broadsides? Dr. Samuel Ball, who conducted the first evaluations of "Sesame Street," believes that the series was bound to be victimized by some because of its success. In Australia, he observes, "we have what we call the 'tall poppy' syndrome. When you see a tall poppy, you saw off its head, quick smart.... The USA is not barren of this kind of reaction to success, either."

There are precious few genuine educational innovations in our country, and "Sesame Street" is one of them. The series' research record clearly supports its effectiveness: "Sesame Street" boasts votes of approval from the 16 million children who watch the show each week, as well as their parents, who witness their children learning from the Muppets, the music, the animation and the characters treating each other with respect and good humor. Personally, I'd take 100 eager kids watching "Sesame Street" over a few disgruntled academics any day.

Myth no. 4: If my child watches TV, she'll be a poor student.

Fact no. 4: It depends on what and how much she is watching. Students who watch a moderate amount of television, especially educational TV, can be excellent students.

The research on this topic will surprise many. Dr. Keith Mielke, senior research fellow at CTW, has examined reviews of research on the relationship of TV viewing to academic achievement.

The studies point out what is commonly touted: Very high levels of TV viewing (35 or more hours per week) negatively correlate with academic achievement. This makes sense, as children who are watching excessive amounts of television do not have time to do much else. But several studies found that academic achievement was positively related to a moderate amount of TV viewing, on the order of 10 to 15 hours a week.

The real issue, Mielke says, is not the sheer number of hours a child watches but what programs she's watching—and how parents and teachers use programs to help maximize learning.

Probably, children who watch 40 hours of TV or more each week are not watching much educational fare. It is also likely that kids who watch a moderate amount receive some strong parental messages about what to watch as well as what to do with the rest of their time, with an educational focus.

Myth no. 5: If my child watches TV, he won't become a good reader. TV and books are enemies.
Fact no. 5: Quality children's programs can actually motivate children to read books and lead to a love of reading.

This curious and widespread belief holds that TV viewing is antithetical to book reading and that kids who watch television will not be good readers. I believe this myth is tied to a larger cultural bias: an intellectual snobbery, in favor of books and against TV.

Joan Ganz Cooney, originator of "Sesame Street" and founder of CTW, clarifies the issue: "Thoughtful people would not argue that because children read comic books, they should not therefore do any additional reading in school. Yet they apply a similar argument to the medium of television."

This pro-book, anti-TV bias doesn't stand up against the evidence of specific TV shows, such as "Reading Rainbow," that encourage the reading of books. After viewing this program, children are so excited to get their hands on *Reading Rainbow* that librarians and bookstore owners report dramatically increased circulations and sales. In one study, 86 percent of children's librarians said the series was responsible for increased circulation. Mimi Kayden, director of children's marketing for E.P. Dutton, has said, "Books that would sell 5,000 copies on their own sell 25,000 copies if they're on "Reading Rainbow."'"

This phenomenon occurs with just about every other popular children's TV show with book and magazine tie-ins. Publishers understand this synergy between TV broadcasts and book sales very well, which explains the many children's books based upon popular characters on children's TV.

A series of *Ghostwriter* books, published just a year ago, has already sold thousands of copies. *Sesame Street* children's books have been best-sellers for more than two decades. *Sesame Street Magazine* is a leading magazine among families with preschoolers and is accompanied by the excellent *Sesame Street Parent's Guide*. Book classics such as *Anne of Green Gables* enjoy renewed sales when their stories are televised.

This phenomenon is certainly not limited to children. Ken Burns' *The Civil War,* Bill Moyers' *Healing and the Mind,* and James Burke's *Connections,* each based on a PBS series, have been best-selling books. After watching a particularly innovative or moving TV show, viewers want to read a book related to it.

Myth no. 6: If my child watches TV shows that entertain as well as educate, he'll expect his teachers to sing and dance.
Fact no. 6: Even young children understand the separate worlds and conventions of TV and the classroom.

One of the strangest myths about children's television is that children who watch Barney and Big Bird will set unrealistic expectations about their teachers' dramatic talents. There is no research to support this notion, nor do teachers report pupils urging them to break out in song or do a little soft-shoe while at the blackboard. Even preschoolers understand what behaviors are appropriate for which situations. I know of no reports in which a child has pointed a make-believe remote at a teacher and attempted to click him off.

Do quality children's programs delude children and their parents into confusing "entertainment" with "education"? Media pundit Neil Postman, in his book *Amusing Ourselves to Death*, contends that this is exactly the problem with educational shows such as "Sesame Street" or "The Voyage of the Mimi," an award-winning series on science and mathematics.

Education, as Postman defines it, is what goes on in the traditional classroom—teacher at the head of the class, students dutifully listening—and entertainment is what television does, using celebrities, music, animation and other cheap thrills. To him, the two are like oil and water.

Education is much more than mere "schooling," but too often we have squeezed the passion and excitement from learning in the classroom. We have disconnected many subjects, such as history, science and art, from the true sense of joy and curiosity that animates the historians, scientists and artists who have made professions out of them. Sadly, we have made learning dull.

Our job as parents and teachers should be to make learning joyful, stimulating and, as George Leonard says, ecstatic. In our culture, there is a strong belief that learning is serious, hard work.

But the way to get young children interested in embarking on this process is to expose them to the joys of learning early on. If television can help in this regard, so much the better. When we label "Sesame Street" or "Nova" as simple "entertainment," we ignore the ways in which TV programs can use video technology and appealing characters to reveal the compelling nature of a subject.

Instead of condemning television for communicating this revolutionary idea, we should focus on making other educational experiences more lively and engaging. The best children's museums and science centers do this. They are places where kids want to go, where they are learning while they are actively engaged with exhibits, museum staff, teachers, parents and one another.

In the end, learning is a voluntary activity. Whether we're 6 or 60, we can't be forced to learn. TV viewing in the home is also a voluntary activity, something your children do because they want to, for positive as well as not-so-positive reasons. The fact that children like TV is something we can build on. When television is well designed, it can appeal not only to their funny bones but to their hearts and minds as well.

Milton Chen is director of the Center for Education and Lifelong Learning at KQED-TV in San Francisco. This essay is reprinted with permission from his book The Smart Parent's Guide to Kids' TV *(KQED Books, 1994).*

13

"Ask Beth"

Elizabeth C. Winship

A couple of years ago I wrote: "Kids used to write me about acne, bras, long hair (boys'), short hair (girls'), nylons, tube tops, 'Mom makes me come home at 9:30!' and 'Should I kiss a boy on the first date?'"

Now they write me about venereal warts and condoms and suicide and drug addiction and "Mom makes me come home at 1 a.m., and none of the other kids have to!" and "Should I sleep with a boy on the first date? I'm 13 [12, 11 or even 10] years old."

These dilemmas illustrate why any normal American teen-ager would write to a newspaper or e-mail a columnist instead of asking Mom or a best friend. From my perspective, teens today not only face situations that are more serious and complicated than they were 30 years ago, but they are confronted with them at ever-younger ages. Young people seem to get depressed to the point of suicide more often. Drug use is so common it's practically part of the culture. Sexual activity is *de rigueur,* and sexual harassment a modern-day plague. The information highway hasn't provided kids with all the answers; even in the information age, there are still some facts they need but are too embarrassed or too scared to discuss with anybody they know. It's easier to ask a faceless person who will neither judge nor ridicule them.

I started writing my syndicated column, "Ask Beth," in 1963. It has always been aimed at teen-agers, the bulk of letters coming from junior high school students. Their main concern is, and always has been, how to attract the opposite sex. "There is this certain boy," many letters still begin. "How do I get him to notice me?" Sometimes, after the 30th such query in a week, I'm tempted to say, "Stand on your head on top of your desk and he'll notice you all right." But you can't be flippant at the expense of these tender young correspondents. So I go on giving tips about being attentive, interested and a good listener. You can't make people like you, but you can get them to see you exist.

When my column first began, kids asked questions like, "My mother won't let me wear nylons!" and "My boyfriend keeps hugging and kissing me in public! I told him that it is embarrassing, but he keeps forgetting." Such problems seem rather quaint today, when nylons are practically unheard of, and students make out in the halls and practically everyplace else.

But what they wear and how they look still matter to practically everybody, but never more than at the junior high and high school stage. At the very time that kids are most insecure about their appearance, they hit puberty and all *those* changes. Noses sometimes grow faster than faces. Hair is too frizzy or too straight. Skin erupts. Voices change. Bodies evolve almost overnight from a straight child's shape to a curvier or more muscular figure. This has always upset teens. Perhaps even more today, considering the media's insistent promotion of the perfect, model-like physique.

Many girls equate a more mature figure with being overweight, so an alarming number of them start rigid diets and develop anorexia or bulimia, like this teen: "I can diet most days, but then I find myself pigging out on ice cream or pizza or chocolate. It's like I'm a food-alcoholic! So I make myself throw up. Sometimes I take laxatives. My friends say I'm sick. Am I?" It's almost impossible to change this obsessive behavior without help, so my advice is to call one of the agencies that deal with eating disorders.

Health problems always are popular topics. The big job for columnists is to figure out which ailments are a normal part of growing up and which ones require professional treatment. All columnists call on medical professionals constantly, and they have advised us of some positive developments that can help change teens' lives. Not so long ago, acne was the scourge of both boys and girls. In 1982, a girl wrote: "I have these *terrible* pimples. It's no picnic. I have no social life. People say I'll outgrow them, but *when*?...Gruesome." But since the advent of benzoyl peroxide, Retin-A and Accutane, I practically never hear about this anymore. The other affliction that still distresses some teens is bed-wetting. A new hormonal treatment called DDAVP has had good results for people with this excruciatingly embarrassing condition.

Hair is also an ongoing topic. But 25 to 30 years ago it wasn't *girls'* hair that caused problems: "My boyfriend has long hair. He got kicked out of school because of it, and now my parents won't let me see him either. I'm going crazy, I'm so lonely.... Despair." The "hippie" look scared parents: "I don't see why my parents care so much what I wear. I like grungy old pants because they are soft. But it drives my mother bananas. How can I make her see it's up to me what I wear?...Leila."

These days, parents and clothing manufacturers copy the teens' costumes as soon as they appear, making it hard for kids to stake out their own territory. Miniskirts, bell bottoms and platform shoes used to be popular with teens, but now they are worn by the most stylish women you see, while kids are into baggy instead. Two bits, that's what will be the rage next among trendy adults.

The need for approval is universal and everlasting. It's also one of the toughest problems to advise kids about. Few adults face anything as agonizing as being out of the popular loop in high school. A girl wrote: "I'm very depressed lately because guys pick on me because I'm ugly. I'm 14 and have never had a boyfriend. Probably I never will! My best friend has an intense relationship with a guy and I'm jealous and unhappy. How can I feel better about myself?...Depressed." Teens are extremely rigid about what constitutes "looking OK." In a different school or a different part of the country, this girl might do just fine.

Then came this letter from another girl that could help kids like "Depressed." "I'm writing to that girl who cried herself to sleep every night. I cried, too, over insults I received in junior high. I was flat-chested and skinny and had short hair and thick glasses. I was shy and self-conscious until I finally decided to stop worrying about what others thought of me and just be myself.

"In high school I got involved in the Special Olympics and Christian Youth Ministry. I ended up editor of the school newspaper and captain of the cross-country and track teams. My advice: Stop crying and enjoy your teen-age time. Guys who are only interested in appearance aren't worth it.... No Name."

This letter illustrates another point that most of us sob sisters soon learn: Advice from other readers is often the most pertinent and helpful of all. This is especially true in issues concerning teen-agers' emotions.

A teen wrote me years ago: "I feel like I've lost *me*. Who *am* I anymore? I'm not a child, but I'm not a grown-up, either. I can't ask my mother. I can't ask my friends. I guess I have to find myself all alone!...Lost." Other teens reading this no doubt felt relieved that their confusion and distress were shared; hearing it from "Lost" was undoubtedly more soothing than anything I could have written. Factual information such as where to call for help is obviously useful, but so is knowing that your peers share your same doubts and fears.

The growing problem of safety is becoming a major teen topic. Teenagers in the 1960s didn't write much about shooting (except for shooting up). Now rising violence has reached into our schools, and the letters reflect teens' fears. School is a different, more dangerous place. Seventy percent of the nation's largest school districts have installed metal scanners to detect weapons—up from 25 percent two years ago, according to the National School Safety Center. This fall I've received many letters like the following: "I'm 13 and I'm scared to go back to school. All I hear about is kids having guns and knives. I'm scared of drugs and I'm scared of the gangs."

I would be scared, too—kids are getting shot by kids every day. What can I say? I urge students to stick together with friends, to find out what the school authorities are planning regarding violence and to get their parents involved. But I'm not sure this makes them feel much safer.

The enduring major topic concerning student relationships is, of course, sex. I get some beauts: "I don't know much about sex. I hear kids talking about things I don't dare admit I don't know about. Like they keep saying so-and-so is impudent. Is this dangerous? Can I catch it from somebody?...Not Knowing." And this one: "Kids tease me because I don't have any pubic hair. My friends say virgins don't get it. Is there any way to get pubic hair without losing your virginity?... Zeke." And this: "Everyone in my class has had sex except me. I'm sick of being the only virgin around. I want to experience an organism like everyone else.... B.J." But most of their questions are not humorous.

I started writing more frankly about sexual issues back in the early 1970s after Gene Patterson, then editor of the *St. Petersburg* (Fla.) *Times,* told me that I was the only columnist tackling this topic for teen-agers. He said I should concentrate on this subject alone. I didn't want to write *only* about sex, but I did start devoting one column a week to "Sense About Sex" (Patterson's title); Thursday has been "sex day" ever since.

I soon discovered that we in the United States still have pretty Victorian ideas about sex. As parents, we either won't or can't educate our kids about sex, but we aren't sure we want schools teaching it either. Only slightly more than half of our students get any kind of sex education. Then we are shocked and surprised that our adolescents get pregnant or—worse—contract sexually transmitted diseases or HIV/AIDS. We continue to warn our children that sex is bad and dangerous, but to an age group that is experimenting with all kinds of "grown-up" actions like drinking and smoking, telling them to "just say no" is practically an invitation.

This subject seems to be endless. Kids write that they want to "get over" their virginity, as if it were a cold or the flu. They write, "Dear Beth, How come every time you meet a boy and you start to talk with them and be with them, they always want to have sex?" and "I really like boys and feel like dying if I don't have a boyfriend. So when I have one I sometimes go really far with him. If my mother found out, she would be very angry." Kids now feel pressure to hop in bed with somebody before they even reach puberty. My advice is Wait! Wait! Wait! But I can't compete with what's on TV and everything else that says, "Do it! Do it now!"

My God, the media broadcast "just say *yes!*" around the clock, day in and day out. Ads for perfume show nearly naked adults about to "do it." Jeans advertisements on 40-foot billboards and in magazines and newspapers show kids clad in skin-tight pants in the most titillating stances. Movies and TV leave nothing to the imagination. How can kids resist?

Current statistics show the results. Approximately one-third of 15-year-olds have had sexual intercourse. Over 30 percent have had four to six or even more partners. More than one million girls under age 20 get pregnant each year, more than 80 percent of them by accident. The number of teens giving birth is rising—over half a million in 1990.

I try to give factual answers to questions about all facets of the subject of sexuality. I used to get some highly critical responses from adults. Not anymore. Some of the more conservative, straight-laced local organizations even ask me to come and speak to their members. Many, many people thank me for telling their children "the facts" because they hadn't known how or were too afraid to raise the issues themselves.

I was on a lecture circuit with a lovely 20-year-old woman who was HIV-positive and just starting to get symptoms. She figured she must have gotten infected five years before in one impromptu encounter with an older man she scarcely knew. Her one aim in what was left of her life was to tell teen-agers the horror of facing illness and disfiguring symptoms and pain and death at an early age. Her courage was inspiring but heartbreaking. This is a constant worry: How can we wake teens up to the danger of HIV/AIDS?

I write endlessly about condoms, how easy it is to get them and how you must use them. There's plenty of proof that *not* using condoms is disastrous. Three million teens a year—one out of six—become infected with a sexually transmitted disease. The incidence of AIDS cases among teen-agers is low, but since it takes eight to 10 years for the HIV infection to develop into full-blown AIDS, the number of HIV-positive teens is undoubtedly very high.

I also regularly receive heart-rending letters from homosexual kids: "Dear Beth, I can't stand my life anymore. I'm gay and everyone hates me. I sat up on the roof of our house all last night, but I'm too chicken even to jump off. Help me!" I was taking written questions from a class of high school freshmen, when a gay student wrote to ask if he should come out to his classmates. So I asked the class what they thought. Unanimously they said, "No way. His life wouldn't be worth a nickel if he did."

When will we accept that differences in sexual orientation is a fact of life and present in all cultures? We must cease encouraging other children to abuse gay people. But for now, the only advice I can give is to find a gay support group, probably in the nearest college or university, or call a gay national help line.

Sexual harassment is growing at an alarming rate in schools today, a direct result of the rise in violence and overt sexuality. "Women's Lib" didn't stop young males from making remarks to their female classmates. Now boys go much further, and snatch and grab at girl students. Occasionally girls harass guys, too, mostly verbally, but it's painful either way. New federal rules make it mandatory for schools to protect students from such harassment. I exhort students to inform their teacher or the school authorities, or at least their parents, right away.

Letters concerning family breakups and divorce, single parenthood and stepparenting are becoming more and more common. "My parents have been separated for three months. I thought I was used to the idea, but when I visited Dad recently I felt as if we were total strangers." Although many teens would never admit it, being apart from a parent is painful and confusing. "I lived with my Dad when my parents got divorced but then he died, so now I'm with my Mom. I'm 14 but she acts like I'm a little kid. She can't trust me. She says Dad spoiled me. How can I tell her anything when she doesn't listen and just gets mad?" When I get this kind of letter, I wish I could write to the parent directly.

Children of divorce can adjust well when their parents cooperate on how to raise them. But letters abound about parents who fight instead or involve the children in their battles, which can create unbearable—even unlivable—environments for their children. "I'm 13 years old and I live with my Mom. My Dad doesn't send child-support money. I am afraid that this will soon start interfering with my personal life (guys and schoolwork)." It's almost impossible to give useful advice to a child when the problem is the parent. I make pleas for parents to consult marriage counseling, but there are no easy solutions. I hope the parents will read my suggestions, but no one appreciates gratuitous advice.

The most important thing advice columnists must learn is to recognize whether they really know the answer. Guessing is dangerous. Moralizing doesn't work. Factual information or wise suggestions usually do. I try to visualize what kids' problems are like—What matters to kids? To be cool, to be popular—and then try to reply in terms of the kids' own lives. I try never to talk down or make fun at the expense of these fragile egos. Many of their problems aren't that much different from those of adults.

Life is pretty desperate out there for our young people. And I've come to the sad conclusion that the main culprit is us—the media—especially television and its new electronic brethren that bombard impressionable young minds. Much of what our children see is tasteless and sexually provocative.

There has been a huge lapse in taste and morality in the media. Do we really want to give our young people the message that sex is OK any time, at any age and anywhere? I'm no prude, but if we keep going in this direction, we can only blame ourselves for the rising numbers of pregnant teens, child mothers and rising incidence of sexually transmitted diseases among teens.

We don't need censorship. We need good judgment, good taste and some real concern about the examples we are setting for tender and impressionable young hearts and minds.

It's the media, stupid!

Elizabeth C. Winship has been writing "Ask Beth," the nationally syndicated question-and-answer column for teen-agers, since 1963. She is the author of The Parents Guide to Risky Times *and* Human Sexuality, *among other books.*

14

"Sesame Street" and Children in Poverty

Keith W. Mielke

In the late 1960s, the founders of "Sesame Street" made a conscious commitment to serve the educational and social needs of children in poverty, not to the *exclusion* of other children, but specifically to the *inclusion* of children in low-income homes. And not as a surrogate or replacement for any other form of educational or social service, but as an added value.

Perhaps the most universally recognizable of children's TV programs, "Sesame Street" now has a quarter-century's experience behind its founding rationale and innovative management strategy. If properly understood and applied as an important thread in the fabric of educational issues, there is even more that can be done to leverage the power of television in the service of preschool education for those who need it most.

Who *does* need it most, this added value in preparing children for the successful transition to school? A cluster of terms has emerged over the years to describe the target populations—"poor," "underserved," "underprivileged," "disadvantaged," "economically deprived," "minorities," "inner-city," "geographically isolated," "at-risk" and those in "ghetto areas of the great urban centers." Each term spotlights some attribute of the target population. Each may carry unintended evaluative connotations as well. One common element, however, is poverty. While a "one size fits all" concept is unrealistic, the income variable is a powerful first cut of the deck and a key to grappling with further subdivisions, such as low-income minorities.

Household income level is linked to level of educational opportunities for the preschool child. Parents with high educational aspirations and the financial means to realize them are more likely to enroll their preschoolers early in high-quality child care and to provide them with a variety of developmental aids, such as age-appropriate books, toys, software and video. Children in high-income families also watch "Sesame Street," and benefit from it, but even if this were not available, their parents would still have on tap these many other means of helping their children prepare for school. Low-income parents, on the other hand, who also want the best for their children, are less able to afford the same range of educational materials for the home. High-quality child care may be not only unaffordable, but unavailable at any price. If a household is in poverty, regardless of the other demographics, there is less likelihood that the parents themselves will be well educated, that the home environment (e.g., safety, nutrition, parenting skills) will be as conducive to early social and cognitive development that is needed as preparation for school, or that the general community support systems (schools, health care, security, museums, libraries, opportunities to participate in cultural events, etc.) will be adequate. For these low-income families with low redundancy of educational opportunity, "Sesame Street," as a free and universal service, can make not only a contribution, but an unduplicated one.

The goal of reaching *all* segments of society plays to the natural strengths of television, by far our most inclusive and heavily consumed medium. Television's power is thoroughly acknowledged in such fields as advertising, politics and journalism. Fortunately, that power does not disappear when the medium is used in the service of preschool education to aid cognitive learning and social development for all preschool children.

The special efforts to make sure that low-income families are included in the audience and are benefiting from the experience are a major part of what makes "Sesame Street" distinctive as a project. These special efforts include the use of expert advisers on the needs of low-income and minority children, continuous feedback research from low-income and minority children, and outreach to low-income communities.

The advisers and the research help shape the series itself (i.e., its content and production) and the development of its educational goals. Part of this shaping over the years has involved the representation of minority groups, people with physical disabilities, females and certain occupations. Spokespersons for groups such as these recognize the power of television and are concerned with the frequency, fairness and realism of their group's television portrayals. They seek a diversity of positive role models on the screen. In this domain of on-screen representation and positive role modeling, the "low-income" variable typically yields in television production to more readily portrayable attributes such as race, gender, age, ability and role. The educational benefits of this role modeling, however, extend with particular relevance to low-income viewers. Although still an underinvestigated research area, the evidence is converging on the importance of identification and positive role modeling to children's self-concept and self-esteem. Furthermore, a wide range of on-screen portrayals can help children develop an attitude of appreciation and celebration of diversity.

Keeping score on television's responsiveness to these needs for representation is not a precise science, nor do we have fixed standards of judgment. Nevertheless, numerous content analyses show that for children's programming, "Sesame Street" and other children's shows on public television portray a much greater diversity of characters, and in more positive roles, than a child will see on commercial broadcasting. "Sesame Street" has always featured a racially diverse cast in an inner-city setting and has always modeled the appreciation of cultural differences. Given the vast needs for representation, this is an ongoing and expanding effort. In recent years, "Sesame Street" has gone beyond "passive" positive modeling into specific goals for explicit teaching and learning about race relations. Four years of expert advice, in-house research and production design have been devoted to developing race relations curricula about African Americans, Latinos, Asian Americans and American Indians.

CTW's management plan for "Sesame Street's" service to low-income viewers does not end with the broadcast of the show. The television series is universally available, and special outreach efforts are targeted to low-income communities. The two efforts work hand in hand. The television series uses the outreach efforts to make sure that low-income households are benefiting. The outreach efforts use the popularity and universal recognition of the television series to open doors and form alliances.

In the early years of "Sesame Street," outreach, particularly to inner-city minority neighborhoods, was essential for reaching low-income households, where there was little tradition of viewing public television. This low-income, minority audience had to be built from scratch, and this was accomplished through a remarkable combination of methods, including neighborhood viewing clubs managed by "block mothers," posters, cruising sound trucks, speeches, services to day care centers and alliances of many kinds.

Initially conceived as part of the general promotional function, it was quickly realized that reaching low-income minority communities required special expertise. That realization led to the separate CTW division of Community Education Services (CES) that has been operating ever since. Natural experiments in the first year showed that awareness and viewing of "Sesame Street" were substantial in low-income communities served by CES, but less so in other low-income areas not yet reached.

The goal of CES's outreach was much more than the promotional task of getting low-income children to watch. It involved working directly with parents to reinforce the belief that the early years of life were educationally critical, that their children were eager learners and were in fact learning something all the time and that the home was their children's first school and the parents their first teachers. Building on parents' natural love for their children, CES tried to give parents specific examples of how they could help and what they could do with the resources they already had. For example, "Sesame Street" has segments that deal with the notions of "same and different"; ask your child about "same and different" when you're sorting the laundry and matching the socks. Outreach, then, does promote viewing and follow-up use of "Sesame Street" as a means to a larger end that involves adult training and improving the learning environment for the preschool child. "Sesame Street" concentrates on the children; outreach concentrates on the adults and community resources in low-income areas.

Outreach is a labor-intensive, local activity not operating under the same economies of scale enjoyed by nationally distributed television programming. At a minimum, outreach requires a network of contacts with potential "customers" in low-income areas. It requires the flexibility to make countless accommodations to highly variable local conditions, even if nominally the outreach is operating under a single banner.

The power of partnerships and alliances has also been an essential feature in serving low-income families. One natural set of partners for "Sesame Street" outreach has been the local public television stations committed to serving low-income populations in their communities. Other alliances have been formed with national and local organizations unrelated to educational broadcasting, but already related to preschool education and children's well-being.

Reports from the "trenches" indicate that a critical managerial tactic for negotiating effective alliances is to avoid issues of turf and ego and to emphasize the win-win common ground. A paraphrased approach might be: "We in 'Sesame Street' outreach can help you in Organization X to reach your goals. We can provide materials and training to supplement what you already have, and we can help you connect these to the familiarity and popularity of the 'Sesame Street' television series. We don't intend to tell you how to do your job or raid your territory or seek to siphon off your funding. We are here to help for as long as you find it useful and invite us to stay." While such arrangements might not make the headlines for "Sesame Street" outreach, they are powerful and effective partnerships for a common goal.

These principles were established by CTW's Community Education Services more than two decades ago: Know the local community, involve parents and care givers; build educationally on the natural love of parents for their children; go beyond promotion of viewing to utilization training for preschoolers; form partnerships and alliances in areas of common goals; and make synergies with the popularity of the television series.

These strategies foreshadowed CTW's development and the 1991 launch of the "Sesame Street" Preschool Educational Program. "Sesame Street" PEP works through local partners such as Public Broadcasting Service stations, child-care professionals and community organizations. The basic idea is to connect the viewing of "Sesame Street" with related readings and follow-up activities in a systematic and sustained manner, reinforced with special training and materials. For many low-income child-care settings, these synergies provide new levels of educational value for the children, as well as professional pride and identification with the role of "teacher" for the staff. The "Sesame Street" PEP effort is expanding and has already trained more than 23,000 child-care professionals, reaching about 221,000 children.

In turn, "Sesame Street" PEP has been a major force and precedent in the recent launch by PBS of its "Ready to Learn" service, which aims to expand similar processes of outreach to the entire block of PBS preschool programs. The phrase "Ready to Learn" is drawn from the first of our six national educational-achievement goals, called "GOALS

2000." By the year 2000, every child will come to school "ready to learn." This phrasing seems not to hit the mark exactly, in that children are *born* ready to learn. Children learn all the time; the issue is *what* they learn. If the phrase lives on, however, there will be a silent translation in the back of many minds to a more appropriate wording such as "Ready for School."

The special efforts to serve low-income children are costly. CTW's heavy use of advisers, the continuous research feedback provided by the target audience, low-income kids themselves, as well as the enormous investment in outreach, are distinctive but not inexpensive features. Are these efforts working? Are they worth it? The cost-benefit equations would be very difficult to state in quantitative terms in the first place and, if so established, would be even more difficult to actually calculate. Therefore, the justification relies ultimately on CTW's mission statement and the conviction that these efforts are the right thing to do. The slate of accountability is by no means blank, however; there is a growing body of evidence about the reach and impact of "Sesame Street" among low-income viewers.

The earliest trend data reporting on the reach of "Sesame Street" in low-income and heavily minority populations came from the Yankelovich research organization's surveys of four inner-city communities served by CTW's outreach efforts—Bedford Stuyvesant and East Harlem in New York City, Chicago and Washington—in 1970, 1971, 1973 and 1978. By 1978, viewing of "Sesame Street" had grown to a point where seven of every 10 households with preschool children reported having seen the show "today or yesterday."

In 1989, as "Sesame Street" turned 20, Yankelovich researchers expanded the scope of the assessment to a national scale, focusing exclusively on low-income whites, African Americans and Latinos. Again, the show's reach was high, with reported viewing of more than 90 percent for the previous two weeks and more than 60 percent for "today or yesterday."

National Nielsen audience ratings provide other indications of the show's reach to low-income households. In a six-week period in early 1994, according to Nielsen, its reach among households with a child under 6 was about the same in households with annual incomes under $20,000 (70.5 percent) as it was in households with incomes over $50,000 (71.9 percent).

A large-scale national survey commissioned in 1993 by the U.S. Department of Education's National Center for Educational Statistics (NCES) has a similar conclusion about reach: 75 percent of preschoolers in the lowest income category ($15,000 or less) watched "Sesame Street," and so did 74 percent in the highest income category ($75,000 or more).

Although falling short of scientific criteria for proof of cause/effect relationships, the NCES survey found some encouraging linkages with "Sesame Street" viewing. For example, preschoolers from poor families who were current "Sesame Street" viewers showed more signs of emerging literacy than did their counterparts who were not viewers. Some of the educational advantages associated with "Sesame Street" viewing were stronger among low-income children than among high-income children, which is consistent with the view stated earlier: In a home with relatively few educational advantages, "Sesame Street" can make an unduplicated contribution.

The pieces of evidence cited above are all frozen in time like still frames pulled from a movie. To see the movie itself in research terms would require focusing on a group of low-income households and following them for a long time, recording as much as possible over and over, and seeing how things turn out over time and in context. Because of an unrestricted grant to CTW by the John D. and Catherine T. MacArthur Foundation, CTW was able to fund such a longitudinal study at the University of Kansas, where Aletha Huston and John Wright co-direct the Center for Research on the Influences of Television on Children. They have completed a three-year study of media use and impact among a panel of low-income families. Their results, which will still take months and even years to digest fully, already suggest that educational television programming such as "Sesame Street" can have a significant impact among low-income children who might otherwise not have equivalent opportunities.

This leads to a powerful rationale for using mass media as part of the mix in serving the developmental needs of children, particularly poor children. Rapid changes in the structures and technological features in the mass media themselves, however, may affect the ability to sustain this strategy. Visions of an information superhighway and a 500-channel environment, about which hype and reality are distributed in unknown proportions, are already changing the way media systems are being thought about. As an experimental "workshop," CTW must explore these new media opportunities. But there is also a growing concern about what the changing media environment might mean for the long-standing commitment to serving the needs of low-income children. One doesn't have to project into "Star Trek" imagery to get the point: The more things cost, the less access there will be for people with low incomes.

Stopping far short of the cutting edge of high technology, one can see that this is already happening. The broadcast version of "Sesame Street" is available to almost every household in the United States and, as cited previously, it reaches low- and high-income households in high and virtually equal proportions. Contrast this with how income differentiates access to two other technologies that have already been around a long time: cable and VCRs. Nielsen data for 1993 show that cable is in fewer than half (45 percent) of U.S. households where income is under $15,000, but in 79 percent of households with income of $60,000 or greater. VCRs are in 44 percent of the under $15,000-income homes, but they're saturated at 96 percent in the $60,000-and-up homes.

The lower strata of income are increasingly becoming the lower strata of access to media services, and that's a problem not yet adequately conceptualized, much less solved. Will we develop some form of entitlement scrip for access to communication technology in low-income households? Will there be an attempt to at least keep local schools and child-care centers modernized with the latest technology, regardless of average community income? Will there remain a strong "free" television structure, available to everyone, for educational series like "Sesame Street"?

"Sesame Street," through its design and management process, its research and its outreach, is reaching and helping low-income children who have a narrower range of educational opportunities in the critical preschool years. This program and educational television generally are important elements in a national strategy for reaching our educational goals for the year 2000. If the true cost-benefit analyses could be calculated—not only for what we gain when we succeed educationally with young children, but also for what we lose when we fail—the case would be even stronger for ensuring that these powerful tools remain universally available, even as new communication technology gets increasingly beyond the reach of the poor. Furthermore, history portends that serving low-income children through the power of media will have to depend on something other than raw market forces to make it happen.

Keith W. Mielke is senior research fellow at the Children's Television Workshop. He thanks CTW colleagues David Britt, Evelyn Davis, Pamela Green, Gerald Lesser and Valeria Lovelace for their generosity in reading drafts of this manuscript.

15

Teaching Media Literacy—
Yo! Are You Hip to This?

Renée Hobbs

Walking down the corridors of a middle school in suburban Massachusetts, the distinctive blare of a television commercial stands out against the more traditional patter of classroom noises:

Yo! Are you hip to these? Are you in the know?
Cause here's where Eggo Minis are made to go—
In Yo' Mouth!
Who needs a plate?
In Yo' Mouth!
Cause they're made to fit your face!
In Yo' Mouth!
They're mega-yum.
In Yo' Mouth!
The taste is pure fun!

Inside the 7th-grade classroom, a teacher is leading a discussion about this particular TV ad; on the blackboard, a list of all the computer graphics and other images in the ad—more than 30 different descriptions—appears on the blackboard, written in a student's handwriting.

"Who's the target audience?" asks the teacher.

"Boys—our age," responds a student. "They only showed boys in this ad."

"And the music—it was like rap music, sung by boys," chimes in another. "It's sung in a kind of aggressive way, and the words 'In Yo' Mouth'—that reminds me of '*In Yo' Face!*'"

"What's a synonym for 'In Yo' Face?'" asks the teacher, feigning ignorance.

The class erupts in laughter, and a chorus of replies follows as children call out their synonyms. The teacher flips open the thesaurus and adds some additional words: defiance, bravado, dare.

The teacher changes the pace. "In your notebooks, everybody take five minutes and write down one or two reasons why the producer chose this phrase for the Eggo Mini Waffles campaign." Notebooks fly open, pens are located and students quickly get down to writing. This is clearly something they have been doing regularly. After five minutes, he asks students to read their ideas aloud. Six hands are in the air.

A dark-haired girl begins to read. "The producer wants to show that eating Mini Waffles is a way of showing independence, being defiant."

Says another, "The producer wants kids to think it's cool to eat breakfast on the run, not with a plate, not sitting down."

"The producer might want to link Eggo Mini Waffles with the attitude of 'In Yo' Face!' because that daring attitude is so popular with kids nowadays," says another boy.

After a few more such interpretations, the teacher wraps up the lesson. "So sometimes commercials can use people's feelings—like defiance—to link to their products. For your critical viewing project tonight at home, I'd like you to look for a commercial that uses bravado, especially kids defying adults. If you find one, write down the name of a commercial and be prepared to describe it to us tomorrow."

Then, the teacher switches gears to *Flowers for Algernon*, the short story the class has been reading, and notes Charlie's growing defiance toward his new friends at this point in the story. The whole media literacy enterprise this day, clearly a regular part of this middle-school English classroom routine, has taken up about 10 minutes of the period.

In more and more classrooms in the United States, educators are beginning to help students acquire the skills they need to manage in a media-saturated environment, recognizing that in its broadest sense, "literacy" must include the ability to skillfully "read" and "write" in a wide range of message forms, especially considering the dominance of image-based electronic media. In fact, the powerful concept of literacy was the driving force that led leaders in the media literacy movement to adopt a comprehensive definition of media literacy as "the ability to access, analyze, evaluate and produce communication in a variety of forms" in a conference sponsored by the Aspen Institute in 1992. Put simply, media literacy includes the skills of literacy extended to all message forms, including those little black squiggles on white paper. Media literacy encompasses reading and writing, speaking and listening, critical viewing and the ability to make your own messages using a wide range of technologies, including audio technology, billboards, cameras, camcorders, and computers. But media literacy is not a new subject area, and it is not just about television—it is literacy for the information age.

Educators find numerous reasons to introduce media literacy as part of the curriculum. Some see it as a tool to build relevance into contemporary education, building links between the classroom and the culture so that students will see how important themes and issues resonate in popular culture just as they do in the study of literature, history or social studies. Some see it as a citizenship survival skill, essential to be a thoughtful consumer and an effective citizen in a superhighway-driven media age. Some see it as a kind of protection for children against the dangers and evils engendered by the excesses of television, and they also see it as an antidote to manipulation and propaganda.

Others see media literacy as a new kind of English education, learning to appreciate and analyze ads and sitcoms and films with the same tools used to study poetry, the short story and the novel. And then there are those who see it as a way to give children the opportunity to tell their own stories and better understand the power of those who shape the stories of our culture and our times.

But there are other visions of media literacy, more narrow and more problematic. Unfortunately, some see media literacy as an option for low-performing, underachieving students whose interest can be piqued by television and nothing else. Some see it as a kind of vocational education, where kids can learn to make TV and head for careers like the grown-ups they see on the screen. Some see it as a chance to play with sophisticated electronic tools, like character generators, video toasters and wave-form monitors. Still others see media literacy as a way to make children aware of the web of "false consciousness" that capitalism has woven into our psyches. Some think media literacy is just about making "good choices" about what to watch or read. And many simply think the curriculum is already too crowded and teachers already too incompetent, burned out or overburdened to make room for media literacy. It is because American educators have so many diverse perspectives on the benefits and value of media literacy and the best strategies for implementation within public education that its last 20 years of growth have been so slow.

Outside the United States, by contrast, media literacy has gained some measure of official status; within Great Britain, Canada, Australia, Scotland, Spain and other nations, it is a required part of language arts programs in grades seven through 12. Most of the training U.S. teachers now receive is strongly patterned after models provided by British scholars, including Len Masterman, David Buckingham, David Lusted and Cary Bazalgette, as well as British and Canadian teachers who have written about their experiences teaching media analysis and media production to young people.

With this nation's renewed interest in children and education in the 1990s, there have been significant signs of recent growth in the movement emerging in the United States. In the state of North Carolina, for example, media literacy is included in both the communication skills (English) and information skills curricula. In many communities, educators have begun the process of thinking seriously about expanding the concept of literacy to include media. While there was only one teacher-training program in media literacy in 1993, in 1994 there were 12 different programs held across the United States. In most communities, however, media literacy exists due to the energy and initiative of a single teacher, not because of a coordinated, communitywide programmatic plan of implementation. The community of Billerica, Mass., is developing a comprehensive media literacy program that reaches all students across the curriculum in grades K-12.

At circle time in a kindergarten class, the teacher shows the children two samples of television programs: an ad and a cartoon. "How are these different?" she asks.

"The first one was shorter," says a little brown-haired girl.

"The first one had real people and real cereal," says a boy.

"The second one was a cartoon," says another.

The teacher notices that her students do not spontaneously use the word "ad," "commercial" or "advertising," so she introduces the words to them: Ads are messages that are trying to sell a product. Over the next few days, they look at a few ads, and after each one, the teacher asks the children to describe how the ad tried to sell the product.

"By making it look real big," says one girl.

"By using music to make it exciting," says another. "By having a story with cartoon animals and birds."

Then the teacher invites a parent into the kindergarten to make a home video of the kindergarten. The parent tapes about 10 minutes of the morning class. At the end of the day, the children watch the tape and sit, transfixed in rapt attention by the familiar images of themselves and their classmates made novel by the camera's presence.

"Did this tape show everything that happened in our class today?" asks the teacher.

Heads nod in agreement. "Yes," they intone in unison.

"It showed us putting our coats on hooks."

"It showed Tim and Kimitha in the loft."

"Was there anything that happened in our class that was not shown?" the teacher asks again.

The children look thoughtful. Arthur raises his hand slowly. "I came in late today," he says. "It didn't show *me* putting my coat on the hook."

Gradually, a flurry of hands go up. All the children can think of things that weren't shown. The teacher carefully listens to all the responses and explains to the children that a camera can never show everything at a scene. She notes, "A camera can only ever show *part* of an event, and it's the person who uses the camera who decides what to show and what to leave out."

While media production is not offered in every school, most have production facilities or equipment of some sort. Videotaping student sporting events and dramatic performances has been routine since the 1970s. According to teachers, it's coaches who often have the most modern video production equipment and playback facilities. And, of course, parents are out in force with their video cameras documenting school plays, recitals and all gatherings that highlight their children's genius.

Student-generated production activities are found less frequently in American schools but are more and more evident at the secondary level, where students, instead of reading the ubiquitous morning announcements over the PA system, may create their own morning news program. High school students make their own music videos, tape commercials for their school plays, perform satirical "Saturday Night Live" skits in after-school programs, deliver critiques of the new principal using computer publishing programs, and hand in class assignments (and college entrance essays) on videotape or via modem. Of course, student production in journalism and the performing arts has long been an important part of secondary education.

In a culture that values technology as the mark of progress and the completion of professional quality media programs as a sign of success, "doing stuff" with video (or better yet, with computers and video) is sometimes touted as cutting-edge education. It is for this reason that educators often jump on the media technology bandwagon. But student-based media production activities do not necessarily build media literacy skills. Sometimes, adults' preoccupation with media technology, and their own ego investment in the product, interferes with a child's engagement in the complex process of learning to create meaningful messages.

One young teacher working with 8- to 12-year-olds eagerly showed off the students' final videotape in a public screening at a private school's summer arts program. It was a satiric takeoff of "Planet of the Apes," with students taking the on-camera roles and reading lines obviously scripted by the teacher. The camera work, editing, sound effects and music selection were all clearly the work of the teacher, someone who was undoubtedly headed for graduate school in film production. Conversation with the children participating in the program revealed that they learned quite a bit about taking direction from a filmmaker, but little about the process and skills of filmmaking itself.

It's not surprising that in an educational environment that values product over process, media production classes (in both print and video) can become playgrounds for creative grown-ups who make all the important decisions about the construction of the school newspaper or class video project, then set young people on the task of finishing the scut work. Many young people who are disillusioned or cynical about student journalism programs in high school point to their inability to take real responsibility for the choice of message content in the paper. Similarly, plenty of video magazine programs are produced by students who are coerced into making promotional messages for the sports program, the foreign-language program, or whatever programs the grown-ups approve. Such is more or less standard educational fare in our schools.

Such practices occur because to truly empower children and youth with the ability to design the content and form of their own messages would entail tremendous risk to the current educational system. The issues that concern our teen-agers today—sexuality, classism and racism, drug use, violence, the environment and the nation's future—are topics that most educators are unprepared to bring into the classroom. Teachers and parents in a community often find the voices of young people very uncomfortable to hear and nearly impossible to respond to.

One of the biggest failures of contemporary journalism education has been in defining its mission as the cultivation of interest in the profession, focusing on developing young people's interests in careers in journalism. This goal is far too narrow, considering the oft-expressed and imminent danger of losing the next generation of news consumers. Journalism educators must begin to carve out a larger and more productive goal, one that reaches all our children: helping young people develop the citizenship skills to be effective, skillful and critical news readers and viewers. Such skills are essential for full participation in a democratic society, yet they are skills that few young people get the opportunity to develop. When newspapers are used in American classrooms, too often they are used for vocabulary practice and reading comprehension, and not to strengthen students' critical understanding of newsgathering practices, their reasoning or analytic skills.

As an effort to reform current educational practice, media literacy advocates explicitly aim to link the skills of analysis with student production activities, in many of the same ways that language arts educators link reading and writing as interdependent skills. But what exactly are the skills of analysis? And what kinds of media analysis are most appropriate for children of different ages? Most media literacy programs stress the following key concepts, adapted from British and Canadian educators:

- *Messages are constructed.* The construction process is invisible to the readers of newspapers or the viewers of television. Awareness of the choices involved in the making of media messages sensitizes readers and viewers to the subtle shaping forces at work—in the choice of photo or cutline in a newspaper, in the images, pacing and editing of a TV news program. Noticing the construction of a message helps one become a more critical, questioning reader and viewer—but this kind of noticing doesn't come naturally to the process of reading or watching TV. It is a learned behavior.
- *Messages are representations of the world.* The reason why media messages are so powerful is that viewers and readers depend on them for their understanding of the culture. One reason why children are thought to be more vulnerable to media influences is because they have less direct real-world experience to compare with the representations provided by television and mass media. Are police officers really like the guys on "Cops"?

Are high school students really as cool as the ones on "Beverly Hills 90210"? Is our community really as dangerous and violent as it appears from reading the newspaper's Metro section? Understanding how media messages shape our visions of the world and our sense of ourselves is a central concept in media literacy.

- *Messages have economic and political purposes and contexts.* Understanding that mass media industries sell audiences to advertisers is a powerful new concept to many American adults, who are barely aware of how a newspaper can be delivered to the doorstep for 35 or 50 cents a day or how television can enter the home at no cost at all. Teaching this concept to young people, of course, can be sticky, for how you teach about it depends on your ideological perspective on advertising, market economics, the industrial revolution and late-20th century capitalism. Individuals employed by giant media companies might not feel comfortable with the idea of high school teachers and students analyzing their ownership patterns and acquisitions, looking critically at their annual reports and reading their trade magazines. But any meaningful critical discourse about media messages must include a careful and systematic examination of the economic and political contexts in which films, TV shows, newspapers and news programs are produced.

- *Individuals create meaning in media messages through interpretation.* While a U.S. family still may occasionally sit down to watch a TV program together, the meanings they derive from the program will differ. Based on contemporary scholarship in literature and the humanities that examines the intersection between the reader and the text as the source of meaning, this perspective focuses on recognizing and critically analyzing the pleasures and satisfactions that readers and viewers get from the experience of media consumption. For example, in one English class, a 10th-grade student submitted an essay on "The World Wrestling Federation," analyzing the powerful symbols of good and evil embedded in the setting, costume and music of the program, interpreting the typical impotence of the referee as a defense of vigilante justice, and describing his own comfort in knowing the good guy will always win. After reading this young viewer's thoughtful, creative work, who can say that WWF is trash television? While not being completely relativistic, media literacy advocates often refuse to line up with those individuals who have a more traditional perspective on children's TV, those who are very comfortable intoning the merits of public broadcasting and the evils of popular, mass audience fare, championing the "good" shows and decrying the "bad" shows. It may not be so important what you watch, media literacy advocates say, but how you watch it.

For years, many educators (and some parents, too) have stood like ostriches, sticking their necks in the sand and trying very hard to ignore media culture. To many of us, television was the enemy of the fine arts, culture, history and all that is best about civilization. The reasoning went like this: If only we ignore television, our children will ignore it and all will be as it was before television.

Now that the culture is almost totally transformed by the compelling electronic and visual experiences that enter our living rooms (and nearly all other parts of our daily lives), the ostrich stance seems more and more ridiculous. It's time to face up to the media culture we have created and the media culture we have consumed. It's time that parents and teachers begin to help our children to embrace and celebrate the messages worth treasuring, to analyze and understand the economic and political forces that sustain the media culture, and to develop the skills and new habits we all need to think carefully and wisely about the messages we create ourselves and the abundant messages we receive.

Renée Hobbs is associate professor of communication at Babson College in Wellesley, Mass., and director of the Harvard Institute on Media Education, a media literacy training program for K-12 teachers.

16

Growing Media Smarts—
The New Mexico Project

Kate Moody

Just look across the expanse of sagebrush and cholla cactus around Alamogordo, and it's no surprise that New Mexico was picked for the first A-bomb testing in the 1940s, ushering in a new era of technology and culture in this country. More surprising, perhaps, is that this same desert region has been chosen as the test site to launch another new era in which culture and technology are studied via a pioneering media literacy program.

New Mexico Gov. Bruce King's proclamation of the state's "Media Literacy Day" in April 1994 was official recognition of a new educational enterprise begun nearly two years before, when state education leaders identified understanding media as a new basic skill, as important in a student's preparation as the traditional three Rs. Media literacy, they said, is the ability to access, analyze, evaluate and create messages in various media; they then set out to identify the component parts of such literacy and to figure out how to teach those skills beginning in elementary school. Although many others are working toward similar goals, and Britain, Australia and Canada have developed such programs, never before in the United States has an entire state set such an ambitious objective for comprehensive media education, K-12.

The New Mexico project seeks to solve one of the most vexing problems of our times in this new information age: how to produce critical thinking about the mass media, which dominate our attention and are even said to "construct" our ideas of reality. Understanding exactly how ideas are constructed is one of the important goals of media education.

Basically, New Mexico's media literacy project came about because Deirdre Downs got mad. What shook up the journalist Downs, a life-long media professional like her father, ABC News' Hugh Downs, was a combination of things: Asked to teach a mass media class in Stockbridge, Mass., she was astonished to learn how little young people understand about how the media—which play such an important role in their world and influence them so mightily—are structured, packaged and delivered. The other thing that moved Downs to establish what became the Downs Media Education Center of Santa Fe, N.M., was her reading in 1991 of media critic Neil Postman's *Amusing Ourselves to Death*, which details how America is drowning itself in entertainment media. Added to her own observations as a teacher, the book became an impetus for Downs to help find ways for Americans to become more media literate.

"We want everybody to learn that media are constrained by forms, codes and conventions, and they *do* present values, messages and ideologies," said DMEC chairman Hugh Downs. "It is important that today's students and tomorrow's citizens and voters are given a framework to ask who are the media, what axes are they grinding, and how can audiences negotiate meaning and interpret what is presented?"

Schools must prepare "tomorrow's citizens" for life in a nation where they'll receive most of their news and entertainment from television—where the TV's "disembodied voice" tells them how to vote and what to buy. A media-literate citizenry—aware not only of the potential effects of mass media, but of how they operate and are structured, what constitutes "good" or "bad"—will yield benefits not only to society but to the media themselves, Hugh Downs argues. "If we had a whole generation of media-literate people, the networks wouldn't have to pander to the arena audience who likes blood and dirt," Downs points out. Perhaps that is what Walt Whitman had in mind when he said, "To have great poets there must be a great audience."

New Mexico was selected as the pilot state for the first National Media Literacy Project for several reasons. First, it has a racially diverse population that parallels what experts say will represent the U.S. population by the year 2000. Public school students speak English, Spanish, Zuni, Navajo. But whatever language is spoken in the home, the language of media is dominant—all students share the pervasive mass media environment, and the need to understand it.

A second reason to site the project in New Mexico was its sparse population of 1.5 million—smaller than Denver—organized into only 88 school districts, which made a statewide program manageable. A relatively poor state, New Mexico cannot fund expensive new programs, which makes it a reasonable model for other states also feeling the financial pinch.

Third, communication studies were already a part of New Mexico's mandatory secondary-education curriculum; although the mandate for "Communications in High School" had already come down from the state, no program had taken shape. So when Deirdre Downs called and explained how and why the communications objective should be expanded to an interdisciplinary media literacy curriculum, she says, it took state Superintendent of Education Alan Morgan "about 20 seconds" to endorse the objective: "We'll be the first media-literate state!" New Mexico's labor secretary declared that "media literacy is a labor issue" and offered his support, and Gov. Bruce King publicly endorsed the project.

Coming to terms with the goal of media literacy means more than just vouching for the concept. Beyond simply accessing information— whether through traditional media or new high-tech options—students must learn how to sift the material, how to question it, analyze it, develop the insights to think critically and make sense of it. Educators differ as to how to achieve such critical thinking.

The New Mexico program is committed to a final outcome in which students produce their own media messages, such as videotaped news stories or commercials. This combination of hands-on knowledge with analytical skills is what may distinguish the pedagogical path of the New Mexico program from others that focus on analysis alone. For some, that is like advocating the teaching of reading without the teaching of writing.

Genuine literacy comes about only when an individual can *both* read and write in a particular medium. Our involvement with the printed word over the last several hundred years tends to make us think of reading and writing alphabetic language in a strictly linear way, on paper, with one word and one thought following another. But we might think of reading and writing in many other media forms, using different perceptual and technical tools to "read" and "write" in different languages using "alphabets" beyond the 26-character written one.

For example, students who synthesize and express information via the in-school television system at Santa Fe High School learn the grammar and syntax of the medium in the process of doing the production, contends teacher Consuelo Gonzales. "Production work involves, engages and empowers students," she says. "They learn the process of meeting an objective having many steps as well as teamwork, organizing, meeting deadlines, quality control and responsibility. These are needed skills for students entering the workplace."

For students who may struggle with traditional, print-based curricula, video and other media can be a richer, more productive new world. "We've experienced the blossoming of many students who lacked confidence in their abilities when allowed to express themselves in other ways," Gonzales says.

Las Cruces, N.M., home of New Mexico State University but essentially a farming community of 100,000 in the southernmost part of the state, is the focal point of the New Mexico media literacy effort, largely because the entire community has embraced the concept. "Media literacy is the talk of the town," says Sunny Conley, owner of a local public relations firm and member of the Las Cruces Media Literacy Steering Committee. "It's almost a household word.... Our town is learning to view media critically, to analyze it, and to judge how it impacts our values, opinions and, ultimately, our daily lives."

At Las Cruces's Hermosa Heights Elementary School, teachers like Ellen Saige help children think about what they see and hear in the media. Kindergarten children talk about characters being "real" or "not real," and what that means, and about the difference between acting in a movie or doing things in real life. Second and third graders examine newspaper ads and news articles and discuss what messages were being sent—fact or fiction. One class watches a video produced by high school students and, after criticizing it robustly, creates its own version. Fourth graders research, write and shoot a video about New Mexican history. Other fourth grade classes watch the video and critique it, recommending changes and additions. Fifth graders study consumerism, creating a video commercial for "Super Goop," in the process learning firsthand about running cameras, and advertising demonstrations and claims. In the high school, students study more advanced television production and the nature of the medium and the TV business—computers and performing arts are important aspects of the curriculum.

Early on April 8, 1994, five school buses from across Dona Aña County converge on Las Cruces's Oñate High School to help the state and Deirdre Downs celebrate New Mexico's Media Literacy Day. "Las Cruces!" she exclaims to a packed auditorium of students, state and local officials and New Mexico media representatives, "You are AMAZING!

"You are doing something here that no one else in America has ever done! Media literacy is important because it comes down to who's going to control our lives."

In a running dialogue, two Oñate High students, Joe and Jason, explain why learning about the media has been important to them:

Joe: "To be media literate you need to get your hands on media."

Jason: "Getting your hands on media means getting your hands on a VCR, computer, newspaper, camera or other media source."

Joe: "Yeah, and it's very important to get different points of view."

Jason: "And once you get these points of view you need to know how they're slanted and how to judge them."

Joe: "And the last step toward media literacy is to know how to make your own media, by writing for the newspaper or making your own video pieces...and this is important because you have ideas for other people to know about. A media-literate person knows how to get a message out."

It was the beginning both of a day of presentations in Las Cruces by media professionals about what they do and why they do it, and of a continuing media literacy effort across the state of New Mexico that is becoming a national model.

The questions raised by the growth of new electronic media technologies and their impact on society and culture have yet to be explored fully. In the relationship between technology and knowledge, Hugh Downs has some reservations. "There's much more data transmission per unit of time than there was. To what end is all this speed being applied?" he asks. "What is it doing to society and education and for enhancing life quality?"

Without a population more savvy in the ways of the media-swamped society in which they live, Downs is pessimistic about the question of quality, whether in life or media content. "If readers and listeners and viewers can become more literate—in the fullest sense—the demand for better fare will grow," he predicts. "It is of utmost importance that people in a democracy be able to read and write: illiteracy in a population is stultifying, blinding and costly. A new kind of literacy is called for in this era of many kinds of media.... The importance of comprehensive media education can hardly be overestimated."

One seed for growing a more media-literate, adaptable, employable, responsible and knowledgeable citizenry has started to sprout in the sands of New Mexico.

The social potential of such a society is enormous, argues Deirdre Downs. "Access, analysis, evaluation and production of information are not just words," she says. "They hold the key to employment, critical thinking, responsible action and peaceful coexistence in a multicultural environment."

Kate Moody, an adjunct professor at Hunter College, City University of New York, where she teaches a course on education and technology in the elementary school, is author of Growing Up on Television.

IV

Kids Making Media

17

Symposium IV

Jana Eisenberg

Six expert witnesses—including two 13-year-old Duluth writers—combine to introduce Part IV, which scrutinizes the disconnect between media for kids and media produced *by* kids. In leading off "Kids Making Media," four expert witnesses—a 19-year-old newspaperman from New York, a radio system president, a Yale scholar and the coordinator of a prominent kids' newspaper section—join our two Minnesota sisters in describing some of what makes news *by kids, for kids* better.

Erin and Julia Hart, 13, writers, New Moon—The Magazine for Girls and Their Dreams, *Duluth, Minn.:*

Let's get straight to the point. The popular media are ignoring girls and who we really are. They tell us what we're supposed to be like and portray our lives as revolving around makeup, celebrities, boys and clothes. Stereotyped views of girls are so common that most people don't even think they're wrong. These stereotypes make girls doubt themselves and feel like they don't measure up. It keeps girls from speaking out.

On TV sitcoms, we see the stereotypical girl talking on her phone, fretting about who's going to take her to the next school dance. But what about girls playing sports, enjoying math or being creative? On the news, everything we see is about disasters like fires, plane crashes, the Cuban refugee crisis, teen-age murders.

We are frustrated. Where are the *girls*? The only girls we see, if any, are victims. We are getting the message that either girls aren't important enough to mention or we haven't done anything! Girls and their lives are interesting and important. So why don't we see this in the popular media? Partly because we don't have a say in creating the popular media. There should be more opportunities for us to participate in the media and voice our opinions.

Bill Zimmerman, special projects editor, Newsday *and* New York Newsday:

In the three-and-a-half years since *Newsday* started our Student Briefing Page, we have received more than 95,000 letters. This reflects a hunger in young people to be taken seriously by newspapers.

While I have seen more newspapers creating special pages and sections geared for kids, few take the time to take kids' intellectual interests seriously and explain news events to children—too many are all fluff and fun 'n' games. In addition, editors in chief have not yet taught their supporting editors to ask the question, "Is there a story on our daily budget list that talks to young people about their events and questions that are important to their lives?" We need to get this thinking into the newsroom, in the same way we have become more sensitive to the needs of minorities and women readers. In addition, with few exceptions, newspapers have not yet come up with enough features written by young people, such as movie or book reviews. Why should adults only be reviewing movies that are produced for kids? Let's get the kids in the paper, too. And why shouldn't kids' views appear on our op-ed pages?

Newspapers must fulfill their responsibility to play a greater role in empowering young people for their future lives—you empower people by giving them information to help them understand the world, and by encouraging them to express their views and offering them a safe haven in our pages for their views to appear.

Edward Zigler, Ph.d., director of the Bush Center in Child Development and Social Policy, Yale University:

In my 30-odd years of tracking social trends, I'd have to conclude that the media have failed children. The nation is just not doing enough for them. If the media were doing a good job at informing people of the magnitude of problems children face, there would be such an outcry that we would see immediate change.

Child abuse is one example. In 1974, there were 700,000 reported cases in the United States; last year, there were over 3 million. Child abuse can be reduced and even prevented, but are the media interested? The media taste seems to be for sensationalism, stories of extreme, horrifying abuse. Thoughtful stories don't have the requisite pizzazz: There's no zing in outlining the kinds of support families need to function effectively.

Some children's issues have been covered better in the last 10 years. Reporters, many of them women, have done a good job on child care and family leave. Three years ago, ABC-TV's "PrimeTime Live" did a piece on substandard day-care centers. The exposé was followed by a story on the U.S. Senate's day-care center, so the audience could see what good child care looks like.

It seems today's media have foregone part of an important potential role: to teach. Education should not be left to scholars alone. The media have an unequaled opportunity to make a critical difference in social policy construction. Sadly, this is an opportunity the media seem willing to miss.

Christopher T. Dahl, president, Radio AAHS/Children's Broadcasting Corporation, Minneapolis:

TV looks at children as if they are the proverbial ants at the picnic. What we do is fun and entertaining and, in a nontraditional way, educational. Radio AAHS proves that if you provide a good product, kids will in fact consume it. The shows are meaningful instead of mindless. About 80 percent of the songs that we play have some content behind them, from innocuous things like "Smile" or "Say thank you," to messages about what life is all about.

Radio is interactive where television can't be—last month we got over 200,000 calls from kids across the country to answer questions and speak to us about their concerns. Kids use their imagination when they listen to radio in a way that isn't required when they watch television. I loved radio as a kid because when you listened to a story, you had to imagine the visuals.

Our listening audience is split equally between boys and girls, which is unusual. Kids 12 and under make up 19 percent of our population, so it amazes me that my fellow broadcasters don't program to this demographic. Radio AAHS is the only full-time media resource for kids on a

24-hour, 7-day-a-week basis in the country today. We provide kids with a full-time media companion. Our news is good news. That doesn't mean we won't get a kid's point of view from Bosnia-Herzegovina or after the earthquake in L.A. But kids are tremendously optimistic about things, and we give them a hopeful view of the world.

Allen Francis, 19, student at Marymount Manhattan College:

How can the media start to serve youth well? By giving us respect and fair portrayals—by devoting as much airtime to teens who make a difference, serve the community, graduate, or just make it as to teens who kill each other. Violence by youth is a hot topic for news broadcasts, but I don't like seeing my peers escorted in handcuffs every other night—it's as though all the media has to say about teens is that we're out of control.

Another reason for kids not to watch newscasts and read newspapers is that they are almost entirely targeted to adults. They toss out terms without explaining them or giving any background information.

The media also need to take us seriously as producers. The city recently cut the funding to my paper, *New Youth Connection* (a magazine by and for New York City teen-agers). *NYC* is a serious newspaper. Important teen issues are covered: parental abuse, worry about street violence, choosing to stay a virgin, trying to raise money for college. Our readers can relate to *NYC* because it is written by people who are going through what they're going through.

The adult media are always covering each other's business—the *New York Post* might close, the *Daily News* is on strike, the *Times* gets a new editor. Well, *NYC*'s funding was cut. Will someone make us a story tonight at 11?

18

A Voice and the Courage to Use It

Robert Clampitt and Stephen Silha

If news media really want to cover communities effectively, they will need to rethink dramatically how they cover children and children's issues. Like canaries in a coal mine, the voices of American children have for years been signaling DANGER AHEAD! The nation is just beginning to listen. A powerful way for media to "mediate" the future is to invite children to become part of the journalistic enterprise—both as vital subjects and as reporters and editors.

"Kids' issues are not just a 'special interest,'" comments Suki Cheong, 16, a Children's Express editor. "They affect all of us—the youth gangs and violence, the drug culture, teen mothers on welfare. Adults are paying in fear and taxes to salvage the lives of these kids we've neglected."

In a country where 3.9 million children live in severely distressed neighborhoods, where the juvenile violent-crime arrest rate increased by 50 percent between 1985 and 1991, where births to single teens increased by 20 percent and the teen violent death rate rose by 13.5 percent in the same six years, we know that it is critical that children's voices (not just their bullets) be included in the national dialogue. These statistics, along with growing awareness of the rot in juvenile institutions, social services, foster care and education, all signal an emergency that raises deepest concerns about our future as a nation.

In 1985, when the children's news organization Children's Express convened its first national symposium on the media and children's issues (there have been three), not one of the 35 news executives and journalists who participated knew of any American newspaper or broadcast outlet that had assigned a beat reporter to cover children's issues. Yet all of us knew that the news media are *the* vital link between children in trouble and the public, the politicians and the policy-makers.

The media's neglect of children was documented early in a 1976 study by Everette E. Dennis and Michal Sadoff that concluded that even when media did cover children's issues such as problems in schools, they tended to cover them from the perspective of adult administrators and government policy-makers, with little attention paid to children's own experience of school or community. This is still the case.

On the other hand, some newspapers and television stations have done good reporting, with powerful results that illustrate the potential impact the media can have on the lives of children. In 1983, for example, the Gannett News Service and a Gannett-owned television station in Oklahoma documented horrendous abuses of children in juvenile institutions. It took a year, but in the end the institutions were closed. In 1984, *The Tennessean* of Nashville, Tenn., ran a five-month series, "Tennessee's Shame: The Forgotten Children." The governor and legislature acted in response and passed legislation to raise children's "standard of need." In 1985, the Lorain, Ohio, *Morning Journal* committed 25 staff members to an extended series on foster care, child abuse, the courts and a range of other issues.

The *Kentucky Post* in Covington declared 1986 its Year of the Child, and all of the *Post*'s 45 full-time editorial staff were involved in a series that took an unflinching look at child prostitution, abuse in detention centers, kids and drugs, child suicides and the foster care system. "The *Post* dealt with so many issues in such a way that its impact on the community would be effective," wrote the teen editors who awarded the series that year's Children's Express Journalism Award for adult reporting on children in trouble.

The *Indianapolis Star,* where Children's Express produces a full page every Monday, has been moving children's issues to the front page. In 1993, both the *Chicago Tribune* and the *Detroit Free Press* launched initiatives on behalf of children. The *Tribune* vowed to cover every homicide of a child on page one and to tell the human and institutional stories behind each death. The *Free Press* launched a more extensive community leadership initiative, "Children First," which raised money, involved child-welfare organizations, held public forums and published solution-oriented reports and resource lists.

These and other series resulted in very substantial action on behalf of children. Legislation was passed, youth-serving staffs were increased, independent review boards were established and institutions closed, and social service agencies united to tackle the problems. In addition, some staff members of media organizations were inspired to take on roles as community volunteers.

Will children's coverage be another media fad? It's too soon to tell. Beginning in January 1995, public broadcasting and other major partners will launch a two-year, solution-oriented "national campaign to reduce youth violence in an unprecedented effort to promote peacemaking, recognize successful local programs and encourage citizen involvement in community violence reduction efforts." Moreover, the Annie E. Casey Foundation has established the Casey Journalism Center for Children and Families at the University of Maryland, and Columbia University's Graduate School of Journalism has established a fellowship program for Children and the News, funded by the Prudential Foundation, which began in fall 1995.

But most reporting on children's issues still concentrates on tragedy or fortuity. Very little of even the best reporting incorporates the voices of children, so when children *are* included, the stories can come as a surprise. "For me it was weird to see kids that had so many worries," comments Kathleen Hustad, a 16-year-old Children's Express editor. "When I was a kid, I liked watching cartoons, I liked riding my Big Wheel and playing Star Wars. These kids today have to worry about being safe and being inside.... I think a lot of American people have the impression that childhood is carefree, that it's innocent, but for a lot of people it's really not."

For almost 20 years, Children's Express has enabled children and teens to participate actively in dialogues about youth issues—homelessness, poverty and violence, sibling rivalries, teen pregnancy, foster care and institutional abuse, drugs and alcoholic parents—bringing the voices, experiences and concerns of young people to adult and youth audiences through newspapers, books, radio and television, hearings and symposia. Throughout much of that time, Children's Express has also urged the adult news media to provide more and better coverage of vital issues affecting children and teens and to use youth voices in stories about their issues.

At Children's Express' first national symposium on the media and children's issues in 1985, publishers, editors and journalists from every part of the country spent two days learning about stories that they *weren't* covering—youth culture, child care, health and hunger, poverty and juvenile justice. Children's Express reporters, 13 and under, presided over most of the sessions.

Claude Sitton, then editor of the Raleigh, N.C., *News & Observer,* opened the symposium: "As a society, we tend to adore children as individuals, but...we tend to ignore them as a group. Oh, we build schools and we publish children's books and we fill Saturday morning with kids' cartoons, but beyond that, we mostly ignore children. Yet no other group is more vulnerable to misfortune, and no other is more critical to our future.... I know from 35 years of news work that we deal daily with issues that affect children. And yet...we don't focus very well. Stories and editorials fail to connect the issues...to children. We deny Americans the information, the perspective and the initiative to solve the problems that affect children."

Indeed, the media are only part of a larger societal neglect. Children who do not grow up in loving families suffer from a kind of handicap our society has yet to address. Though news media coverage of children's issues has expanded greatly since 1985, still only a handful of reporters are assigned to cover children's lives. Still missing from such coverage, for the most part, are the voices of children and teens, who are clearly experts on their own experience and feelings.

Underlying this exclusion of children's voices when covering children's issues is a cultural perception of children as powerless and inarticulate, as noncontributing members of the community for whom others are responsible or as simply a media "audience" or "market segment" to be lured in with colorful graphics and connect-the-dots puzzles. As Robin Doussard, former features editor for the Fort Lauderdale, Fla., *Sun-Sentinel,* put it, "One of the very basic problems in covering children is that not only are they not free agents, but they're not articulate. We live and die on a good quote."

But that's a gross misperception. Take this example from José, a 10-year-old from Brooklyn, N.Y., whose quotes could easily keep a story alive. "We live in an apartment," he begins. "I like listening to music, and I'm scared whenever I go outside.

"I would love to move out 'cause there's too much violence on this block. Most of the time, I'm terrified. I used to be very active when I was a little kid, but now I'm just scared because my mother cries every night. I never told anybody.

"I don't know what to do because when the violence starts up, we're going to have to fight back," José says. "But I don't want to hurt anyone. Sometimes I count on my friends. But I also count on myself. There's nobody else to protect me."

Children's Express editors get good quotes from children every day. Part of the secret, of course, is their age—14 to 18—and their ability to strike up a relationship with younger children. Another part of it, however, is patience and a real desire to talk to kids and listen to them. Adult journalists might be handicapped by their age, but that's not insurmountable. Children's Express editors offer adult reporters the following advice:

1. It helps to believe that kids have important things to say.
2. Don't tower over kids when talking to them. Get as close to their eye level as you can.
3. Make it more like a conversation than an interview.
4. Encourage them to tell you about something that interests them or that they do well. Kids like to talk about good things about themselves, not just the negative.
5. Tell them something personal about yourself as a way to get them to open up about themselves. They may be ashamed of the subject you want to discuss; an impersonal attitude doesn't help.
6. Be prepared to spend some real time with children you interview. If you do, they may give you a totally different insight that is valuable and important.

"Children's Express means to me that we will get the story," says Becky Oberg, 15. "Not only that, but we'll report it through a child's eyes. This is our world. These are our stories." In fact, those stories can be the critical creative spark that gives a community a new slant on a seemingly intractable problem.

Critics sometimes charge Children's Express with publishing too many "downer" stories that do not jibe with their vision of children. But in fact, children gravitate to serious stories, rejecting most stories about products and cartoons as fluffy and patronizing, as they feel most newspaper youth sections are. The organization's mission—to give children a significant voice in the world—evolved from children themselves. The defining moment in the early life of Children's Express occurred at the 1976 Democratic National Convention. Twenty-some young reporters, ranging in age from 9 to 13, entered Madison Square Garden armed with preconvention credentials. The Children's Express publisher, an adult who had launched a magazine with the motto "by children, for children," suggested that the young reporters talk to telephone install-ers, hot dog vendors and construction workers to find out how a na-tional convention is put together. Not one of the reporters followed any of his suggestions.

Instead, the young, T-shirted reporters found members of the national press corps hanging out, testing equipment and exchanging war stories. So the kids interviewed them—Walter Cronkite, Dan Rather, Bill Moyers, Roger Mudd, Edwin Newman and others—and learned from the veter-ans all about delegates and the selection process and the issues before the convention. The only real question, the adult press corps said, was whom Jimmy Carter would choose as a running mate.

Once the convention got under way, the young reporters penetrated Democratic defenses and spent substantial time on the floor. When 12-year-old Lee Heh Margolies asked Chicago Mayor Richard Daley about the riots and demonstrations at the Chicago convention in 1968, he told her that the press had invented the story, giving convention reporters and delegates their biggest laugh of the week.

The major story of the convention was reported by Gilbert Giles, a 12-year-old from Brooklyn who scooped the national and international press corps with this headline in the Children's Express convention newspa-per—"It's Official: Carter/Mondale!"—and became an international story himself. In the process, the young reporters had reinvented Children's Express; instead of "by children, for children," it became "by children, for everyone." We learned that when children are given important respon-sibilities, their confidence and interest in the world around them grow very rapidly. It was clear that children want a voice and that they have much to contribute. As Jessica Trentlyn, then 11, one of the 1976 conven-tion press corps, put it, "I think it's very important that we're finally hav-ing a chance to talk out and tell the world what we really think."

As Children's Express evolved, three kinds of stories emerged, along with a process. The story types include interviews, event reports and dialogues with children about their lives and experiences. The process is called "oral journalism," in which everything is tape-recorded, tran-scribed and then edited by teens, with guidance from adults. In the case of an interview, for example, a debriefing follows in which the teen editors ask questions and the reporters talk out the story—including their own reactions and feelings about what they learned.

What emerges, and what is absent from most adult journalism, is the child's voice and experience without filters. The Children's Express dialogues, or roundtables, are powerful windows into the lives our children are living. ". . . what frightens Patrick is growing up and becoming a monster, a mirror image of his parents" recalls Fedley, 17, a Children's Express editor. "When I finished interviewing, I had to stop. I've never had to stop a tape recorder just to breathe. It was just amazing."

The children's event reporting often takes on a decidedly frank tone. Here, for example, is how a team of four 11- to 13-year-olds reported on Ronald Reagan's first inauguration:

> This inauguration is what the country wanted. This is what they wanted Reagan to do. They wanted him to put on a grand show, and they want some comforting. They want the spirit of it.
>
> It is like a nice spring day. There are mink coats and spiked heels (getting stuck in the mud). And a lot of talk....
>
> America is asking for so much this year that maybe we needed an $8 million inauguration, but I think it was a real waste of money—it should have been used for education or health. It's like a big party. Why look at reality tonight?...
>
> Nancy could feel very proud. Her husband is president and she is first lady. I think she had a lot to do with it. I think she is very strong....
>
> The American people are asking for too much—much too much. The pressure is on him to be perfect.
>
> They're asking for inflation to stop, for it to be the turn of the century again—no more war, America big and strong, women in the kitchen, suburbs all over, everything so nice and peachy-keen. People wanted to go back to *Saturday Evening Post* covers. I don't think Reagan can do that. I don't think anybody can do that.

At least one adult journalist thinks her peers have much to learn from Children's Express. In her Indiana University master's thesis, "Children's Express: Young Journalists Show the Way," Jane Dwyre Garton concludes:

> [T]heir fresh ideas constitute a new voice in journalism that must be heard both for the welfare of a democratic country and, on a very basic, practical level, for the future of the newspaper industry.
>
> This thesis recognizes and endorses the established innovation by Children's Express of using child sources. It acknowledges the child-advocacy mission of the organization that at times leads to the practice of advocacy journalism. It concludes that the advocacy journalism is done openly and honestly—guilelessly, if you will— and represents a type of community leadership assumed by the children.
>
> . . . Children's Express produces a legacy to hand up to adult journalists by showing a persistence to task, the conscience to take a point of view in writing, and the

confidence to identify issues which are ripe for debate and action. These practices...are available to and appropriate for adoption by adult journalists.

Specifically, Garton suggests journalism take four lessons from the Children's Express newsroom:

1. *Staying True to Voice.* "By using tape recorders in every interview situation," Garton writes, "Children's Express journalists have a tool that frees them from the distraction of note taking. They also ultimately have transcripts from which to work. That insures accuracy and encourages the use of the voice of their source."
2. *The Team Approach.* "Because these journalists are children," she suggests, "it is acceptable for them to acknowledge they are still learning. They act as coaches for each other. They work with adults to brief themselves before doing interviews. They debrief after every interview and before they begin their collaborative writing of stories. The team effort offers additional insight and discussion time to young journalists and reassures them that their performance is not a solo act, that it is part of a far more complex proposition—the newspaper."
3. *Taking Outsiders' Input.* "Children's Express routinely invites community leaders to visit and to discuss story topics with them. The tradition is carried out via a monthly meeting, run by the kids, in which they turn to the adults with their interests and ask about resources on the topic. In what is a seemingly simple one-handed exchange, the bridge between the adults and the child media community becomes stronger."
4. *Embracing a Mix.* "An interest in the world—not their school, not their neighborhood, not their previous work experience—brings journalists to the news bureau," Garton says. "Their newsroom is diverse in age range, racial mix and socioeconomic/geographic mix. This diversity provides the team with rich and child-candid discussions."

While Children's Express does not claim to be training future journalists, many of its alumni have gone on to work in the news media. "I realize now that Children's Express techniques gave me a good ear for voice," says Paula Bock, a former Children's Express editor who now reports for the *Seattle Times*. "What is a good quote? What voice should I use to write [someone's] story? I pay more attention to detail, to emotion. I think I'm better able to bring readers into the story."

In the future, interactive technologies will enable more children to express themselves in writing and in broadcast forms. Already, children around the globe are chatting with each other on interactive electronic bulletin boards. They also enjoy the opportunity to chat electronically with adults; in cyberspace, no one can talk down to kids because of their size.

News media can literally "mediate" discussions among children and between children and adults, both on local community levels and on national and international levels, by providing context, teaching civil discourse, asking good questions and giving children a chance to ask their questions in public.

In 20 years of work with children and media, we have learned some important lessons:

- Children are ready to take on more responsibility than adults assume. When they're given responsibility to report on their lives and the lives of other children, they feel powerful and important, and they do marvelous work.
- Children and teens learn and grow rapidly when they are entrusted with important responsibilities. At Children's Express, they develop a wide range of skills they can use throughout their lives, including reporting, editing, writing, research, group leadership, interpersonal skills and training.
- About 25,000 children have shared their experiences, thoughts and feelings with Children's Express editors in interviews or roundtable discussions. The most frequent feedback: "Nobody has ever really listened to me before."
- Children wielding the power of the press provide strong positive role models for other children and teens who see, hear or read them in the media.
- Media are among very few links between children and public policy-makers. Though there is a journalistic tradition of championing children in cases of extreme abuse, there is little ongoing coverage of children in any way comparable to that of, say, city hall.
- Children's issues are not that different from adult issues. The addition of children's perspectives, particularly in areas where they have experience, enhances coverage in general.
- Children have no access to the media or to politicians through lobbying organizations like the American Association of Retired People because they lack both the vote and economic power—so news media coverage comes down to the matter of responsibility, together with the interests of the community and the nation.

Amy Weisenbach was 16 when she talked in 1992 about what working with kids on their own media products had given her. "Children's Express isn't just about reporting for the paper. It's not only about getting kids' voices heard, although that is its main purpose," she said. "Children's Express is about exploring issues. I have learned that I don't have to wait until I'm an adult to think about issues. Children's Express has given me a voice and the courage to use it."

Robert Clampitt is founder and president of Children's Express. Stephen Silha is a free-lance writer and communications consultant who has worked with Children's Express for 10 years.

19

News Advisory—Listen to the Children

Susan Herr and Dennis Sykes

During 1993, each time a child was murdered in Chicago's metropolitan area, the *Chicago Tribune* ran a front-page story. The death count
began when the *Tribune* labeled 14-year-old Tatiana Redmond victim
No. 1 on the first day of the year. The last story ran on Christmas Eve
when victim No. 62, 11-month-old Lauren O'Neal, was beaten to death
by a 10-year-old boy. The series, entitled "Killing Our Children," graphically illustrated the warlike conditions in which Chicago's inner-city
youth live. The *Tribune* devoted significant resources to its coverage,
which was nominated for a Pulitzer Prize, seeking, the editors said, to
"...accord the loss of each young life the significance it deserves and
to see if a detailed knowledge can bring an end to the escalation of
violence against those we have the greatest duty to protect."

However worthy the goal, the quality of this series and most others
that examine the lives of inner-city children is compromised because
editors (and members of Pulitzer Prize selection committees) suffer from
what we call "paternal journalism," the notion that media can provide
readers with "detailed knowledge" about people's lives without including the voices of those people. The "Killing Our Children" series exem-
plifies flaws inherent in paternal journalism as it is practiced by adults
covering children, particularly inner-city children. Although this series
is only one of many possible examples of the kind of paternal journalism that characterizes nearly all mainstream coverage of children, we
use it to illustrate the concept because 1) the 96-page reprint of the
Tribune's yearlong series included only a half-page of quotes directly
from children; 2) its nomination for a Pulitzer Prize indicates that it is

setting the standard for coverage about inner-city youth; and 3) because, as advisers to the cadre of teen journalists who produce Chicago's citywide teen newspaper, *New Expression*, we saw this coverage unfold while in the company of the young people who were being portrayed.

Despite the claim that quality journalism can be objective, fair and balanced, reporters still see the world through the lenses of personal experience. Communicating across the broad differences of race, gender and age in American society is still a hit-and-miss proposition.

The "Killing Our Children" series was received as a gritty, streetwise piece of reporting despite the fact that it was laundered through the filters of race, socioeconomic status and age. The result is a message suitable for an audience that shares more characteristics with its reporters than with its subjects. Consider these facts:

- Although most of the subjects in the "Killing Our Children" series are nonwhite, most of the *Tribune*'s reporters are white.
- The subjects of the "Killing Our Children" series live in some of the worst urban conditions in the United States; the socioeconomic status of *Tribune* reporters is, primarily, middle class.
- The subjects in the "Killing Our Children" series are, by definition, children; the reporters are adults.

As the adult producers of a teen newspaper, we have suffered similar lapses. For instance, when following up on media coverage of the 300 incidents of gunfire at Chicago's Robert Taylor Home in spring 1994, we assigned *New Expression* teen photographers to shoot photos that would graphically illustrate the violence. But the teen residents of the Robert Taylor Homes warned our photographers that they weren't welcome, educating us about the anger they felt because the news media rarely showed the positive side of their community. As a result, *New Expression*'s front-page headline read, "Why Are the Cameras Here Only When Someone Dies?" The page carried photos of four high-achieving high school students from the Robert Taylor Homes and described their accomplishments. Below, the caption proclaimed: "We are ambitious. We are hardworking. And we all live in the Robert Taylor Homes."

This cover received more response than any other we ran last year. Mayor Richard Daley cited the *New Expression* coverage in his State of the City address and invited the four young people profiled to join him for his address.

Through this experience, we at *New Expression* were reminded that when children speak for themselves, it is easy to remember that they aren't simply victims or victimizers—they take on dimensions as girl scouts and basketball players and grandchildren, tap dancers, band members and science-fair winners. We were reminded that stereotypes blind us to the richness of individual human experience. Sadly, that blindness is the norm in most mainstream media coverage.

One justification for paternal journalism may be that children aren't developmentally capable of informing adults about the complex realities that shape the war zone of America's inner cities. But *Anne Frank: The Diary of a Young Girl* needs no adult explanation. Nor does the more contemporary, fictionalized urban film "Boyz in the Hood," produced by John Singleton when he was 21. The young authors of these stories ably communicate across the gaps of race, age, and socioeconomics with their potent messages intact. As a result, they humanize two of the most inhumane living situations of the 20th century. It is important to note that Anne Frank was not a paragon. She was simply a girl like many others, who touched us because she shared from her heart. America's inner cities are filled with young girls and boys whose perspectives carry the "detailed knowledge," as the *Tribune* sought, "that can bring to an end the escalation of violence against those we have the greatest duty to protect," if we only listen to them.

Adding children's voices to mainstream media needn't be difficult. It can be accomplished by creating partnerships with the many youth journalism programs throughout the country that are preparing urban youth for careers in newsrooms. Although high schools should be the best place to develop young writers, journalism programs are often impaired by limited funds or by censorship endorsed by the 1988 Supreme Court *Hazelwood* ruling.

But other models for tapping young journalists and young audiences exist. Founded in 1976, Youth Communication/Chicago Center was the first program to provide high school students the hands-on training that comes from producing a citywide teen newspaper. *New Expression* (circulation 80,000) served as the model for Youth Communication papers now publishing in 11 cities, including New York, Los Angeles, Washington, Atlanta, Boston and Detroit. Written by, for and about teens, Youth Communication papers give young people high-quality information about the topics that concern them so they can make more informed decisions about their lives. Independent teen publications explore the tough issues urban young people face every day, such as teen parenting, recovery from sexual abuse, and explicit AIDS risk-reduction information. They also portray teens as valuable, contributing members of society.

In their efforts to include youth perspectives, mainstream daily newspapers such as the *Los Angeles Times*, *New York Newsday*, the *New York Daily News* and the *Chicago Sun-Times* have utilized copy from the teens who produce citywide publications. *New Youth Connections* (circulation 68,000) has partnered with *New York Newsday* to include teen interviews of Haitian teens as well as first-person pieces on the Ms. Foundation's "Take Your Daughter to Work Day." These pieces have run as part of *New York Newsday*'s "Student Briefing" page. The *Los Angeles Times*, which provides in-kind printing of 100,000 copies of *L.A. Youth* each month, also utilized Youth Communication's teen journalists to explore biracial heritage in a first-person essay and racism through a comic strip. These pieces and others have been included in the *Times*' "Voices" section, launched after the 1992 L.A. riots, in an effort to bring diverse voices into the paper.

In the fall of 1993, the *Chicago Sun-Times* asked *New Expression* reporters to provide a youth perspective to the impact of the funding crisis that closed Chicago public schools, publishing daily opinion pieces by teen journalists for a week. One wrote about how the closing would affect her college-application process; another about losing this last chance to turn around less-than-perfect grades; a third about how the extended summer meant more time protecting her little sister from the random gunfire that permeated her Englewood neighborhood. The *Sun-Times* realized that these perspectives didn't replace facts about negotiations, time lines and budgets, but knew they humanized those facts for the many readers who were affected by the ongoing schools crisis.

Paternal journalism ultimately misses the mark because it cannot fully convey the hopes and dreams of children, and the perhaps naive optimism that allows so many of them to survive and even prosper in dire circumstances. It is neither analysis nor statistics that will inspire adults to wage peace on behalf of children, but rather, the voices of the children themselves. It is their voices that remind us that the more we learn, the less we know. In Anne Frank's diary and in the work of young authors in film and other media, adults can hear anew the power of simple truth. In every American community there are young people who can speak for themselves, and would if we could hear them, and should because we adults cannot. It should be not only the award-winning standard for journalism, but also the social obligation and the privilege of mass media to resurrect the spirit of Anne Frank and others with her kind of simple, powerful insights by including young voices in our newspapers, television and everywhere else that children and adults can gather together and listen.

Susan Herr is the executive director and Dennis Sykes the programs coordinator for Youth Communication, the nonprofit publisher of Chicago's citywide teen newspaper, New Expression.

20

Our Own Voices, Please

Marjani Coffey

It's not always easy for me to find *New Expression*—or *NE*—Chicago's monthly newspaper written for and by teens. This is because my Catholic, college-preparatory high school, unlike most Chicago high schools, doesn't subscribe. I believe this is because *NE*, like most other teen-produced publications, focuses on the real lives of teen-agers without sugar-coating. These are the media through which real-life teens tell their real-life stories, straying away from the romantic ideal teen-ager's life. Instead of columns about how to change your image and the ever-annoying 10 ways to guarantee a prom date, in *NE* teens share their experiences about sexuality, family problems, racism and violence.

Whenever I do run across an issue of *NE*, I devour it from cover to cover. Although I read publications for teens written by adults, publications written by teens have an impact that adult writers can't seem to produce. Adults can write about facts—financing a college education or developing good study habits—but when it comes to writing about the effect a situation is having on *me*, teens do it best.

The column "Momma Said," run in *NE* during the 1993–94 school year, gave first-person accounts of teen mothers and how being a parent affected their lives. An adult could've given some stats on teen mothers, gathered a few quotes, and maybe inserted his or her opinions, but no adult could've given the column the same passion a teenager did. Teenage writers let teen readers feel their pain, experience their joy, understand their position. To people who have never been in that situation, teen mothers became real people and not just statistics taking advantage of the hardworking taxpayer.

Teens all over the country are fortunate to have teen-produced publications in their area. *NE* has, for example, sister publications in Los Angeles (*L.A. Youth*), Boston (*United Youth*), San Francisco (*YO!*), Atlanta (*VOX—Voice of a New Generation*) and New York City (*New Youth Connection*). *New Youth Connection* (*NYC*) featured a first-person account of a teen who decided to lose her virginity and later regretted it. The author told of how her relationship with her boyfriend fell apart and how alone she felt afterward. I'm sure many teens were moved by this piece, as I was, and began to re-evaluate rushing into a sexual relationship. Adults preaching, "Don't have sex until you're married" or "Don't have an abortion" can't yield the same powerful, positive reaction as listening to the heartfelt, sometimes tearful, accounts of their peers.

In the same issue of *NYC*, various teen reporters told how they survived living in abusive homes. Their horror-filled stories came to life and made me more concerned about the role of state governments and their monitoring of children and teens in troubled homes. Reading data and numbers in the news doesn't move me as much as learning from the source the nightmare he endures daily.

When I think about "paternal journalism," I think about adults reporting on how issues affect teens without taking the time to find out how teens think. I also think about how adults report on what they *think* are teen issues, but in reality are issues most teens don't care about—such as how to be "popular" and the latest gossip on the celebrity scene. In either of these cases, "paternal journalism" is more a liability than an asset. Often, teens reading paternal journalism become apathetic and ignore the media altogether because they don't feel it represents their reality.

Adults can sometimes report on teens effectively, but only teens, themselves, can express their emotions and the emotions of their peers. An auto mechanic wouldn't be asked to report on nuclear physics because he has no experience in the field. Why should an adult be asked to report on a teen when he has no experience on being a teen in the 1990s?

Marjani Coffey, 16, is a junior at St. Ignatius College Prep in Chicago and a member of the staff of New Expression.

21

Harlem Snapshot—
Schooling in New Technologies

Josiah Brown

The phone rings in the computer lab of Manhattan's PS 125, the Ralph Bunche (elementary) School for Science and Technology. Teacher and computer maestro Paul Reese answers: "Hi, Renso." At the other end is Renso Vasquez Jr., a seventh-grader from JHS 43, a half-mile away in south Harlem. A 1993 Ralph Bunche graduate, Renso is now helping his junior high—a grant-backed partner of PS 125—to utilize the kind of new technologies he learned about in grammar school. On this day, he is employing an integrated computer/video program that allows users at two locations to see and communicate with each other.

After switching to the appropriate screen on his computer, instructor Reese calls across the room to Ifeoma Anunkor, a sixth-grader who, as she often does, is spending the afternoon in the lab. Together, they turn on and adjust a nearby video camera and complete the link with JHS 43. Waving to Renso, who appears with a classmate in a corner of the screen, Ifeoma takes over in front of the keyboard. She begins a multimedia correspondence that attracts observers from around the room.

The teleconferencing technology associated with this scene may seem routine to many corporate executives. But for the children at the Ralph Bunche School—African American and Latino youngsters from mostly marginal neighborhoods and families of modest means—such technical tools are truly compelling and eye-opening.

For several years, through a series of grants, PS 125 has participated in projects that expose its students to learning vehicles rarely found at such urban public schools, or even at many better-financed institutions for that matter. From a Panasonic-sponsored "Kid Witness News" video journalism program to a spot on the global Internet, the boys and girls at Ralph Bunche have enjoyed innovative educational opportunities. What the students' experiences suggest are not just the wonders and potential of these technologies, but also the consequences if their benefits are not made widely available.

The debate over access, of course, is far from new, having figured in early discussions of cable television well before the nascent informa-tion highway began to evolve. Yet recent developments, including the drafting of congressional telecommunication legislation, have lent greater urgency and import to the access question. Due in part to the activity of advocacy groups, public-interest criteria—the push to wire schools, li-braries, health clinics, etc.—have become one priority in the Clinton administration's plans for the National Information Infrastructure (NII).

While nearly everyone agrees that the private sector will (and should) be largely responsible for advancing and harmonizing the existing elec-tronic pathways, and while an environment of minimal regulatory re-strictions is deemed essential to productive competition, the need for public considerations is recognized. The conflicts are over what consti-tutes that need, how adequately to address it, who pays and how much.

Visiting a school like Ralph Bunche can help illuminate and give focus to these controversies. Moreover, some time with these young people and their modern tools highlights especially vividly the educa-tional promise of new media.

Educators have long touted the academic rewards of computers, if used imaginatively, and the children of PS 125 certainly provide sup-porting evidence. Through inviting screen images, sounds and games, each student is encouraged not only to learn facts but to enhance his or her verbal and problem-solving abilities.

On a typical afternoon, sixth-grader Moses Wallace is engrossed in a game that simulates a time machine, challenging players to absorb key details about the world's cultures and historical eras. Sitting nearby, Nephtali Cruz is intent on his own screen, on which he is busy tackling mystery stories that test his knowledge of geography. He tracks sus-pects from Moscow to Singapore, collecting clues along the way.

Although such edifying computer games have existed for a decade, they are clearly improving steadily in their sophistication and their capacity to engage young minds. Silent, boring, monochrome drills have yielded to colorfully provocative adventures. Given the uproar over the violence-laden "Mortal Kombat" and others of its genre, we can take comfort in how effectively many software designers, noting children's affinity for video games, are actually teaching them something valuable.

"Edutainment" denotes this rapidly growing breed of programs—more than 200 new ones appear annually—captivating countless kids and teens. As economies of scale curb prices and CD-ROMs proliferate, multimedia learning is exploding. Yet the trend has primarily been limited to middle and upper-middle class households, to the estimated 4 million multimedia home PCs. Only a comparatively few school systems—notably in California and Texas—are moving aggressively toward utilization of self-contained multimedia units or, as in North Carolina, Florida and Utah, toward various forms of video/computer networking. Strapped inner-city districts are understandably lagging. Thus the Ralph Bunche case is representative yet in some respects exceptional, an indication of what might be.

The effect on individual students is apparent. Ifeoma is a technology devotee who "loves" the Broderbund geography/mystery game "Where in the World Is Carmen Sandiego?" that her classmate was playing. An editor of the Ralph Bunche newspaper, the *Computer School News,* Ifeoma has been using computers since first grade and affirms that they have reinforced her academic interests and motivation. Although she says that "my mom wants me to be a politician," Ifeoma has not decided on a career. One possibility is to be a reporter or TV anchor "like Tom Brokaw."

In the long run, more significant than the educational games at Ralph Bunche is the students' familiarity with interactive networking. The children of PS 125 are encountering, early on, technologies that will mark the unfolding information age. These youngsters are testing firsthand the kind of tools that are emerging around the country, chiefly—so far—for the relatively few communities able to afford the necessary fees and equipment.

Given that less than 20 percent of classrooms have telephone lines, let alone modems and adequate computers, a universal digital highway is still quite distant, even once basic wiring concerns are addressed. In order to obtain a concrete measure of current conditions, the U.S. Department of Education this fall is joining the National Telecommunications and Information Administration and the Federal Communications

Commission in compiling a survey of telecommunications links in America's classrooms. Secretary of Education Richard Riley, in testimony before the Senate Commerce Committee in May 1994, implied that meeting the goal of universal access would be difficult. He asserted that "free connections to NII may not be enough," that "free usage of the telecommunications lines" for educational purposes, along with further steps, might be necessary.

For those schools that are already connected, free bulletin-board services like FrEdmail (Free Education Mail) and FidoNet's K12Net allow students and teachers to exchange messages; at a cost of several hundred dollars per year or term, classes can pursue more curriculum-directed projects via AT&T's Learning Network or the National Geographic Kids Network, among others. A program called the Global Lab permits international student cooperation in scientific and environmental matters.

PS 125 is part of the National School Network Testbed, which includes initiatives at the national, school-district and intraschool levels. In addition to Internet privileges, the Testbed provides specific forums in areas such as science, math and teacher development. The National Science Foundation has been a principal funder of the Testbed, which continues to grow both in scope and scale.

Returning with a handful of his students from a national education and computing conference in Boston last spring, Reese was exhilarated and proud. Four sixth-graders and two junior-high "graduate assistants"—Renso and fellow lab veteran Hamidou Diori—had wowed the conference with their exhibition of networking skills. Their workshop featured an elaborate series of e-mail messages, back and forth between Boston and New York, along with Hamidou's display of the Gopher server used to navigate the Internet. Now back home in the lab, the students sampled new software and sent electronic mail to people they had met at the conference.

These and other pupils have enjoyed the benefits of Ralph Bunche's Computer Mini-School within a school. Comprising 160 of approximately 700 students, the Mini-School (to which admission is based on a lottery) brings its member classes into the lab for additional time, both for word processing of regular coursework and for special computer instruction. Each child has an e-mail account.

The intense fascination, verging on reliance, that many adults have with e-mail communication is now generally acknowledged; the power that this medium holds for children, however, has not yet been as widely documented. In the Mini-School setting, e-mail has helped Reese and colleagues promote a sense of "community and stability" that has resulted, without deliberate effort, in improved standardized test scores. "I respond to every student [e-mail] letter I get," maintains Reese—up to several dozen every day.

In a reply to an e-mail note that Reese had sent him, one boy wrote, "That lettler [sic] was great. I never knew that you were so intrested [sic] in carpentry.... I know how to work with tools and power tools." In itself, the simple message is hardly earthshaking, but it reflects a level of bonding between teacher and child, and a growing facility with a technology that most adults—inside Harlem or out—have yet to master. The electronic medium can facilitate expression and exchange of ideas, among students, among teachers and between the two groups. And communication within the school is frequently supplemented by meaningful contacts outside it.

At PS 125, e-mail is remarkably versatile. Articles and information for the *Computer School News,* which is composed and available on screen, are submitted electronically. Then there are the opportunities for external communication. Ralph Bunche students have established, and carefully recorded, correspondence with people across the United States and abroad. Whether doing research that requires discussion with a librarian in another state or merely building friendships with digital pen pals, the children transcend the physical confines of their school. Fifth-grader Kenneth Lopez even used e-mail to lodge a complaint with President Clinton. Kenneth's concern: why "Take Your Daughters to Work Day" has no equivalent for boys.

One expert who is familiar with PS 125 agrees on the significance of its networking component. Linda Roberts, Education Secretary Riley's advisor on technology, downplays the extent to which the Ralph Bunche School is unusual, at least from the national perspective from which she observes a great deal of innovation within particular districts and institutions. Rather, she stresses PS 125's importance as an example of how electronic networking can be "a facilitator for gathering and sharing information." The interactive possibilities, she asserts, are "making a difference in what [the children] are learning and how they're learning." Paul Reese, she says, is "a pioneer" whose "relentless" efforts have been fundamental. Not surprisingly, her experience convinces her that such deeply involved educators are crucial in any viable classroom technology venture.

It's no accident that Roberts knows about the Ralph Bunche experiment. Because of its technological orientation and resources in its urban location, the school has attracted a rare amount of attention. Educators, journalists and elected officials including Rep. Charles Rangel, D-N.Y., have come to watch the students at work. In May, FCC Chairman Reed Hundt stopped by. Chronicling the incident for the *Computer School News*, 12-year-old Renso concluded: "I guess that Mr. Hundt's visit has raised our confidence.... [It] definitely has made me proud of what this school has to offer. I think that the people at Washington, D.C., were very impressed with us!"

Indeed, Hundt, once a seventh-grade social studies teacher before studying law, has demonstrated a sincere commitment to the access issues confronting industry and Congress as well as the FCC. In a May 10 speech, he argued that in order to replicate PS 125-type capabilities nationwide, "we will need special transmission rates for our schools which do not have the financial wherewithal to pay the absolute top dollar. We will need to make sure that the opportunity to participate extends to all schools."

While a look at PS 125 does reinforce some of the widespread optimism about technology's educational impact, the experience there also evokes the magnitude of obstacles that remain. As important as the hardware is, advanced computers and interactive networks are of limited value without a sufficiently redesigned curriculum that fully integrates them; thus the Mini-School is modest as a model for extensive reforms. In addition, there are the more basic challenges that disproportionately afflict schools in impoverished neighborhoods. At Ralph Bunche as elsewhere, one hears pleas for more generous staffing to ease class size and provide children with more individual attention, particularly those whose behavior reflects social deprivation. And keeping in mind what a recent national study suggested—that students score best in states that spend a high percentage of their education monies on teachers—policy-makers should be wary of primarily technological solutions. Educators understand the need for a more comprehensive approach, but only a fraction of schools have the will and the money to move forward.

Clearly, the power of technology is finite and easily exaggerated; human and fiscal elements will continue to play a major, perhaps deciding, role in the educational equation. Yet irrespective of these vagaries, interactive multimedia tools in themselves are becoming increasingly important, and children unable to share in them will be at a disadvantage. Within a decade or so, most middle-class homes and school districts will likely possess advanced PCs or set-top devices—machines that will enable students not only to become computer literate but to prepare for an information society. In this environment, universal access to the digital highway will be merely a minimum requirement, not a panacea.

Still, it is encouraging to glimpse what the new media might bring. While the results of the digital revolution will remain uneven and uncertain for years to come, there are real, positive dividends to be secured, lively imaginations to be captured—not just frightful scenarios to be avoided.

Late in June, Reese was scrambling to find students to complete the year-end edition of the *Computer School News*. Ifeoma, Rebecca Best and the other sixth-grade members of the staff were busy with graduation festivities. The "graduate assistants," Renso and Hamidou, were elsewhere, and there were no interested fifth graders in the lab. So Reese turned to a couple of bright fourth graders, José Hernandez and Evelyn Lopez.

With surprisingly little guidance, they did the job. Deftly manipulating the desktop publishing software, they inserted photos, wrote captions, aligned margins, made headlines the right size. They made a mistake or two, of course, but José and Evelyn learned quickly from their errors and before long were impressively competent. After three afternoons, the fourth graders' passion and curiosity had prevailed; the newspaper was finished and ready for distribution, both within the school and on the Internet. Confident and pleased with their achievement, José and Evelyn could look forward to the fall even as they savored their summer vacation. The *Computer School News* had two new editors.

This article was written when Josiah Brown was The Freedom Forum Media Studies Center's assistant to the executive director for special projects. He is currently assistant to the president, New School for Social Research.

22

Coming Up Next...A Brighter Tomorrow for Kids' TV

Karen W. Jaffe

In the 1990s, kids came into their own as big business for television. Recognizing the trend lines, trade magazines took note: "TV Industry Sees Brighter Kids Market," proclaimed *Electronic Media*, for one, in a special 1992 report dedicated to "The Power of Kids." Among the "new advertisers coming into the kids' category," said Andy Heyward, president of DIC Enterprises, a major supplier of kids' cartoons, were jeans, consumer electronics, fast food and soft drinks. "Computers have not even come into kids advertising yet," observed John Claster, another children's TV producer. But it wouldn't be long.

PBS's "The Magic School Bus" premiered in 1994 with Microsoft as a major underwriter, following the lead of a major sportswear company, Nike, which helped launch the Children's Television Workshop's "Ghostwriter" several years ago. Underwriting public television is not where most of the money is in kids' television, of course, but in commercial broadcasting and cable, although public-interest advocates worry that advertising takes advantage of young children and that some programs seem like commercials for these products.

Still, even though the new potential riches embedded in the children's market have driven some television producers to well-publicized lows, there are bright spots to report. While some, like the three-year-old Cartoon Network, continue to depend heavily on reruns of previous kids' fare, many new shows also demonstrate innovations in television production. New outlets with different perspectives have created wider variety and demonstrated a new vision for children's programming. Take pay cable, for example, where Disney has developed more drama and long-form shows for kids, Showtime has produced a variety of children's specials based on books, and HBO has pioneered documentaries and docudramas specifically for young children and teens. The new Shelley Duvall live-action series on Showtime, "Mrs. Piggle-Wiggle," recreates the humor and fantasy of the Betty MacDonald books through original sets and costumes that seem to leap off the screen. The award-winning "Avonlea" series on the Disney Channel is filmed with the same depth and expansive period sets and costumes as theatrical feature films. Nickelodeon uses a combination of live performance and expressionistic props for its teen show "Roundhouse," and its animated series "Doug" maximizes the creative style of animation with unusual color and line. CBS's "Beakman's World" combines hilarious sets and comedic characters to demonstrate scientific phenomena, and a new show on ABC, "Reboot," uses state-of-the-art computer animation to tell stories that take place inside a computer. In fact, new technology was both the vehicle and the subject in the 1994 season as the notion of TV in cyberspace can be found across the remote-control "dial"—for example, "Paleoworld" on The Learning Channel, Nickelodeon's "U to U" and "Masters of the Maze" on the Family Channel.

New TV technology is also helping disenfranchised people, including kids, to gain access to shows designed for them. Under the Television Decoder Circuitry Act of 1990, not only must televisions be equipped with caption decoders, but the Federal Communications Commission has broadened the scope of what the decoders can do. Captions may now be positioned anywhere on the screen, can include a larger character set for better support of other languages, and allow for a second stream of captions, which could include edited or "easy reader" captions or even a simultaneous second language. Another technological breakthrough created the Descriptive Video Service, which provides narration for the blind or visually impaired.

The biggest regulatory changes affecting children's programming stem from the Children's Television Act of 1990, which calls for broadcasters to air informational and educational programming for kids. Since last summer's informal *en banc* hearing, it seems clear that the FCC has plenty of recommendations to help develop a policy, even though it took the agency four years and a new administration to decide to implement rules to support the law. Despite all this progress, however, regulations to enforce the Act are still not in place.

While the commercial networks have increased the number of programs that would seem to qualify under this statute in anticipation of the new FCC rules, progress is less consistent at the local level. Some local stations have begun to create their own programs while others purchase recycled shows and still others maintain the status quo. A combination of regulation and market forces is key to quality program development for kids at the local level: If the children's market is as bullish as anticipated, we can hope that advertising dollars will find their way to support quality local children's shows as well as national fare. And, if the FCC mandates a number of hours per week for programs with defined educational goals and objectives, scheduled with continuity and targeted to specific age groups, the advertising opportunities could make the investment in new programming pay off for local stations as well as national networks—and everybody will have to increase the number of quality shows for kids.

What's most important in reflecting on children's television is what kids actually see on the screen. Ten years ago, the superhero/action hero was predominant. Then came the "Smurfs" on NBC, and characters became "softer." Today, programs run the gamut, from "X-Men" and "Mighty Morphin Power Rangers" to "Bobby"s World" and "Rimba's Island," all on Fox. While syndicators have produced shows like "The Superhuman Samurai Syber Squad" and "Monster Force," you can also find "The Little Mermaid," "Aladdin" and "Free Willy." Some try to combine action and education—ABC's "CRO," for example, which is supported in part by the National Science Foundation and uses the adventures of animated prehistoric characters to demonstrate scientific principles.

One area of children's programming that everyone agrees needs improvement is in sex-role character stereotyping. Since research shows that boys will watch only shows with male characters, while girls will watch both male and female characters, very few shows exist that feature strong role models for girls. Judy Price, chief children's programmer at CBS, observes that her Saturday-morning cartoon, "The Little Mermaid," features a strong female character but is lagging in the ratings because boys won't watch it. Price also makes the point that some shows, such as Fox's "Power Rangers," do have strong female characters who "are in control."

One genre that allows for more honest and often controversial messages for kids is the sporadic weekday afternoon drama. In one "CBS Schoolbreak," called "My Summer as a Girl," a young teen-aged boy dresses up like a girl for a summer and learns a few lessons about how to treat women. Nickelodeon's Cyma Zarghami contends that her network tries to develop shows that are non-gender-specific, featuring characters that appeal to both boys and girls and have equal viewership from both sexes. "Muppet Matinee" and "Rugrats," for example, portray genders in balance, as does the game show "Family Double Dare"; in "Clarissa Explains It All," a girl character is the focus, but boys and girls are partners, as they are in "Hey Dude," which takes place on a ranch. And "Nick News" is entirely gender egalitarian. In some cases, family programs that kids watch at night—such as the ever-popular "Full House" and the newer "Boy Meets World" on ABC—offer more realistic role models.

Television may actually be doing a better job in terms of minority representation than gender portrayals. Jenny Trias, president of children's programming at ABC, is optimistic about some minority representation in children's shows, most notably African Americans, although there are fewer examples of Asians, Hispanics and Native Americans. For example, "Cro" is an animated show featuring an 11-year-old African American assistant to an adult Latina scientist. And "Free Willy" focuses on an African American teen girl who aspires to be a marine biologist. ABC's animated series "Schoolhouse Rock," which debuted in 1973 with integrated voices, has now been revised to include characters of various ethnic groups as integral parts of the program, an example of a successful evolutionary process. Then there's Fox's "Rimba's Island," whose focus is Native American culture. Showtime's dramatic show, "Ready or Not," portrays both—positive preteen girl role models in story lines featuring kids of all racial backgrounds; race is not an issue. In an episode called "First Date," the girl character Busy struggles with a budding relationship with a boy named Troy. The fact that Busy is white and Troy is black is never openly discussed in the story line—it's just how the characters are cast. Showtime's vice president of family programming, Lori Kahn, believes that as diversity becomes a more important issue for society, television will reflect and reinforce it. The network is also airing another drama first broadcast on PBS, "Degrassi Junior High"; considered by many to be on the cutting edge, the show regularly deals with issues of adolescent sexuality and moral conflict. Race also has been addressed directly on the Fox Children's Network, which has used the miniprogram format (or 60- to 90-second interstitial) to tell poignant stories. The most recent series to air this season addresses issues of sensitivity, teen fatherhood and manhood, divorce and family, self-acceptance, tolerance, equality and love. These spots, developed in consort with a professional advisory board, take pains to reflect appropriate racial and sexual role models.

In addition to the trend toward "rites of passage" themes in preadolescent and teen programming, there is more honesty and realism in programs targeted to kids. "In the past," says Showtime's Kahn, "storytelling was from the adult's point of view. Now it's more from the child's perspective."

Since adults are still doing the writing, this is often difficult. A large part of Nickelodeon's success, says that channel's Zarghami, is a conscious effort to develop characters that are like regular kids—not the 1980s' amazing kids who had done exceptional things, like the 6-year-old concert pianist or 11-year-old pilot, but "average" kids with whom the audience would like to be friends. Examples include "Clarissa," "Doug" and especially "Rugrats," which uses exaggerated shapes, sizes and camera angles to show the world from the toddler's perspective. "If kids feel good about themselves and if they see kids on TV with the same experiences as they have, their self-esteem goes up," Zarghami contends.

ABC's Trias says the industry is doing a better job in telling stories that present more complete, three-dimensional characters, including story lines that give them more "motive." Some shows actually empower kids, she says. This is the primary theme of the new ABC series "Bump in the Night," which fortifies convictions that there really is something living under the bed, and that toys come to life when children aren't looking. The 10-inch-tall Mr. Bumpy lives under the bed of a young boy and has a tendency to devour socks and car keys, therefore creating predicaments for the unsuspecting humans in the household. Another series of prime-time family specials on ABC produced by Lily Tomlin goes right to the child psyche. In the animated "Edith Ann" series, developed around her famous inner child, Tomlin introduces Edith Ann's thoughts about family, friends and school and even facilitates these perceptions with the help of the school guidance counselor who is both mentor and therapist. One new theme, says Alice Cahn, PBS's director for children's programming, is that "being smart is cool." Two PBS offerings, "Ghost-writer" and "Where in the World Is Carmen Sandiego?" make the point through the use of mystery, suspense, games and puzzles that stress writing skills, critical thinking and geographic knowledge.

PBS has always filled its shows with strong role models for kids. Whether they're caring and teaching adults like Fred Rogers, Shari Lewis or the community on "Sesame Street," kids see adults who listen, who are nurturing and who entertain them on their level. "Sesame Street" was the pioneer in diversity for children's TV, prominently featuring people of different racial and ethnic backgrounds, disabilities, ages and socioeconomic groups: "Sesame Street" made individuality commonplace. Cahn also is concerned that much on television, especially on commercial TV, represents antagonism between kids and adults. This is the case when kids are portrayed as protagonists in a story line and the grown-ups, often parents or teachers, are the ineffective and even dishonest villains. Kids need to see more of a balance, she argues.

Pay channels don't have to worry about advertisers and therefore can take more risks in programming. HBO, for example, has developed several reality-based programs for kids, including a series designed to teach kids about advertising, television, and consumerism called "Buy Me That," produced by *Consumer Reports*. Now available with study guides for schools, this series could exist only on a network that is advertising free. A second series for older kids called "Lifestories" consists of compelling, fact-based dramas about real and often difficult issues. The half-hour show, primarily designed for after-school time periods but often repeated at night, features epilogues in which the characters discuss the results of their actions.

PBS has traditionally owned the field of news and documentaries for kids, but the genre has slowly spread as more reality-based shows for kids, including straight news and newsmagazines, have emerged, mostly due to opportunities on cable TV. But the networks have made some changes in their standard entertainment fare, too. Over the last two years, ABC has produced six live, 90-minute Saturday morning news specials hosted by Peter Jennings called "ABC Answering Children's Questions," and both ABC and CBS have used their after-school special time slot to air documentaries for youth. Syndicators such as Fox have produced newsmagazines like "Not Just News," and even local stations have ventured into the field, though with less stay-ing power. Many cable networks have made a commitment to this genre, usually with the idea that schools could use their programming in the classroom. "CNN Newsroom" is a weekday, 15-minute, com-mercial-free news show that educators can tape and reuse in perpetu-ity; "Assignment Discovery" is a weekday, one-hour, commercial-free documentary series on the Discovery Channel that can be used by teach-ers for one year; Nickelodeon airs Linda Ellerbee's weekly "Nick News" and "Special Edition"; Turner Program Services syndicates "Feed Your Mind," which replaced "Real News for Kids" on TBS and in syndication; Showtime, Disney, TBS, A&E, the Family Channel, even MTV air documentaries or special newsmagazine shows for kids. And the options are growing.

Despite all these and other good-for-kids shows, we're still not there yet. PBS's Alice Cahn worries that there are still way too many things for kids to see in their time periods that "sensationalize stories and have no value for kids," such as talk shows and tabloids.

When I testified before the FCC at its June 1994 *en banc* hearing, one of my recommendations was that the government consider ways to encourage more public/private partnerships in children's television. There are models: Disney's "Bill Nye the Science Guy" aired in 1994 on PBS and in commercial syndication; ABC"s "CRO" was created with money from the National Science Foundation; the musical performance series "Center Stage" was a collaboration between Chicago's public WTTW-TV and cable's VH-1; and the memorable "Avonlea" series on the Disney Channel was originally developed as part of the PBS "Won-derworks" anthology with production help from Disney. And there are many examples of local partnerships, as well.

In addition to action by the FCC toward true quality, more attention needs to be paid to ratings for children's shows, because existing rating systems are not designed to measure programs targeted to specific age groups. A long-range vision must be developed for this market, espe-cially as new, interactive technologies spread a variety of media directly to individual children through computers, on-line services and CD-ROMs. Through partnerships in education and industry, alternative means of distribution—including the emerging interactive technolo-gies—can supply more economic and educational resources for children's content. I have faith in the media industries to use the best of their creative resources to continue to produce more quality programs for children. But will the FCC help them get there?

Karen W. Jaffe is executive director of KIDSNET, a Washington clearinghouse for children's television and radio. Beth Steingard's research contributed to this chapter.

V

Books and Organizations

23

Smarter Than We Think— Kids, Passivity and the Media

Katharine E. Heintz

Television and the American Child
George Comstock and Haejung Paik
San Diego, Calif.: Academic Press, 1991

Big World, Small Screen: The Role of Television in American Society
Aletha C. Huston *et al.*
Lincoln, Neb.: University of Nebraska Press, 1992

Children and Television: Images in a Changing Sociocultural World
Gordon L. Berry and Joy Keiko Asamen
Newbury Park, Calif.: Sage, 1993

Media, Children, and the Family
Dolf Zillman, Jennings Bryant and Aletha C. Huston, eds.
Hillsdale, N.J.: Lawrence Erlbaum Associates, 1994

Playing with Power in Movies, Television, and Video Games
Marsha Kinder
Berkeley, Calif.: University of California Press, 1991

Sold Separately: Parents and Children in Consumer Culture
Ellen Seiter
New Brunswick, N.J.: Rutgers University Press, 1993

Popular magazines are wellsprings of information for people concerned about the topic of children and electronic media as well as a barometer of concern on the topic. In February 1994, *Working Mother* magazine offered "TV Guidance"; in March, *Child Magazine* told parents how to "Put TV in its Place"; *Ms.* warned in its July/August issue, "Caution: Children Watching"; even my local neighborhood parents' newspaper in Seattle, the *Eastside Parent*, described in June "How Television Disables Your Preschool Child." Last March, *TV Guide* provided a "Parents' Guide to Kids' TV," while the April issue of *Instructor* magazine offered tips on "Teaching Television Watchers." The previous September, *Time* warned of the "Attack of the Video Games," which the fall '93 Business and *Society Review* called "the school of hard knocks, knives, and numchaks."

As these titles suggest, the relationship between children and the electronic media worries parents, educators and the general public. This comes as no surprise, since historically the introduction of every new media has been followed by widespread public concern about its potential effects on children. Television has been a focus of such concern since the 1960s and remains so for parents and educators in the 1990s because of its increasingly explicit content, increased channel capacity and use as a conduit for purchased or rented videotapes and video games. Although issues surrounding video-game and television violence captured the headlines (yet again) last year, this is just one issue that worries media researchers and the general public.

The magazine articles just mentioned reflect three main areas of concern about television. First is the amount of time children spend with the medium. At issue here is the belief that television viewing is a passive activity that is not as beneficial for children as active involvement in play or more serious pursuits like reading. Second is the content that children are exposed to, especially its potential negative effects on children's beliefs, attitudes and behaviors; media representations of women and minority group members are thought to encourage stereotyping, while increasingly graphic sexual and violent content are blamed for escalating rates of real-life violence and teen-agers' sexual activity. Advertising is problematic because it targets children too young to be actual consumers and emphasizes consumption as the solution to problems. Third, interventions to reduce negative effects: What can anyone do to "protect" children?

These issues are addressed in six new books on children and media. Four employ a mostly social and behavioral science orientation, not surprising since the vast majority of work in this area has been carried out by scholars in such fields as psychology, sociology and communications. The other two books are representative of the growing influence of cultural studies in this area of research.

Two comprehensive reviews of the literature are available in *Television and the American Child* by communication scholars George Comstock and Haejung Paik, and *Big World, Small Screen: The Role of Television in American Society* by the American Psychological Association's Task Force on Television and Society, headed by Aletha C. Huston. *Big World, Small Screen* restricts its review primarily to research published after the 1982 National Institute of Mental Health report on television and behavior, and its content deals not only with children as audience members but with other "vulnerable" and low-power social groups—the elderly, ethnic minorities and women. Comstock and Paik review, synthesize and in some cases reanalyze data from the 1930s Payne Fund Studies to the present. Their focus is exclusively on research regarding child audiences.

Two edited volumes examined in this essay combine reviews of previous literature with presentation of new research evidence. *Children and Television: Images in a Changing Sociocultural World*, edited by Gordon L. Berry and Joy Keiko Asamen, addresses the role of television's content in the formation of children's perceptions of the social world and their place in it. *Media, Children, and the Family*, edited by Dolf Zillman, Jennings Bryant and Aletha C. Huston, deals with the role of the family in children's media experience. A significant proportion of this book is devoted to discussion of the influence of sexual, violent and sexually violent content on users ranging from teen-age soap-opera viewers to students in college-level communications classes to sex offenders. *Playing with Power in Movies, Television, and Video Games* by Marsha Kinder of the University of Southern California examines the connections between different entertainment media and the ways children use and understand them. Finally, Ellen Seiter analyzes the social and cultural role of advertising directed to children in *Sold Separately: Parents and Children in Consumer Culture*.

American children, born into a media-rich society, go home from the hospital (where their mothers' rooms are often equipped with television sets, VCRs, and even CD players) to multimedia households. Exposure to television begins in infancy and children become "viewers" before their first birthdays. The time spent with television increases throughout childhood, peaking at about four hours per day during grade school before dropping off in adolescence as radio and music take up more of their leisure time.

A common caricature of the television-viewing child is the "zombie," sitting passively in front of a screen whose glowing images have induced a hypnotic-like trance. Contrast this with the idealized picture of the nonviewing child, either reading an enriching book or outside joyfully playing with stimulating toys and playmates. If this scene really did exist for four hours a day in the typical American household, there is no wonder time spent with television is a call for concern. But the research reviewed by George Comstock and Haejung Paik in their *Television and the American Child,* and by Aletha C. Huston and her colleagues at the American Psychological Association's Task Force on Television and Society in *Big World, Small Screen* show that television neither induces hypnotic trances nor replaces more stimulating activities. Obviously some activities are not being performed while the television is on, but studies since the 1960s have shown consistently that activities that are "displaced" by television viewing are those that serve the same purpose—comic book reading, radio listening, "doing nothing." Participation in activities that children deem personally and socially important (like peer play and sports) are not replaced by television viewing, and often they accompany it. Children also often use the television-viewing situation as a background for family or peer interaction. Observations of groups of children or families viewing together show that there is often a great deal of play, talk and touching during viewing. In fact, this social orientation may be a reason TV viewing drops during adolescence, when teens begin to invest less time in family relationships and more in peer relationships.

Children are not only physically active in front of the television set, they are mentally active as well. In their books, Comstock and Paik, and Huston *et al.* review a vast set of literature that shows children are not passive zombies who attend to and absorb TV information wholesale. Rather, children are shown to actively select when, where and what level of attention they will invest in the tube. When toys, other media or other people are present in the TV room, visual attention to the set is generally lower than when there are no such distractors. Children readily divide their attention between TV and other available alternatives.

Children's decisions to pay attention to the television screen are influenced by program content. Attention levels are lowest for content that is either too easy and redundant or too difficult and complex, highest when programs are challenging and somewhat unpredictable. As children grow and have more experiences (both with television and in the real world), they find more things interesting and meaningful. It is not surprising, then, that visual attention increases throughout childhood.

Before a viewer can pay attention, however, she has to look at the screen. With distractors present in the room, how do children decide when to turn their attention to television? Research has shown that children (indeed, all of us) attend to TV's audio track even when not looking at the visuals. In fact, audio cues often signal nonviewers to look at the screen. Stories abound of children running from adjacent rooms when they hear the "Sesame Street" theme song or the voice of Bert, Ernie or Big Bird. Huston and her colleagues at the Center for Research on the Influence of Television on Children at the University of Kansas were interested in finding out what it was about programming that influenced children to watch or look away. They divided TV programming into content and noncontent features, the former referring to plot and story, and the latter referring to production and editing conventions such as zooms, dissolves, music, special effects and pacing. They argue that information is conveyed through both content and noncontent features, and that certain noncontent features are regularly paired with the same type of content and can therefore act as cues for the type of content to be expected. Viewers then use the content and noncontent features when making decisions about whether to watch the action.

For example, anyone who has recently watched children's programs and advertisements can fairly easily distinguish those targeting girls from those targeting boys. Not only are they about different things (content), but they look and sound different (noncontent). Boys are sold toys and programs through themes of good vs. evil and heavy doses of violence or action. Boy programs and ads feature dark environments, quick cuts, loud music and harsh voices. Girls are sold toys and programs through themes of interpersonal sharing and caring, usually set either in fantasy lands or suburban homes, with soft music, pastel backgrounds, high-pitched female voices and slower pacing. Never is there a mixing of these conventions—girl commercials never feature dark environments or good vs. evil themes, and boy commercials never feature pastels and soft music. So while there is no meaning inherent in fast or slow pacing or in color selection, the consistent pairing of these content and noncontent aspects infuses them with meaning. Within the first seconds of a TV commercial, young viewers know whether they are in the target audience, and can make an informed decision whether to pay attention. Huston and her colleagues have found children as young as three recognizing the meaning of noncontent features and using them as cues for attention. It doesn't take long to learn some of TV's conventions.

In *Playing with Power,* Kinder argues that the content and experience of TV viewing need not be pacifying or stultifying, but can be challenging and empowering. She suggests that the remote-control device can be an empowering tool for children. As young viewers become more adept at using the remote to channel surf or to manipulate videotape images, they discover that they have power over the images. They can "zap" undesirable images and endlessly replay pleasurable scenes. In this way, Kinder suggests, television teaches children that spectatorship can be fun and interactive.

Kinder also proposes that the nature of many children's programs makes them challenging, thus stimulating attention and creativity. Programs designed for children are highly intertextual, she argues, borrowing content and forms from movies, advertising, video games and television's own various genres—music videos, soap operas, etc. For example, she describes an episode of "The Muppet Babies," an animated series that "consistently presents a running commentary on the relationship between movies and television and how they train youngsters to read narratives interactively." In the episode she describes, the Muppet Babies (and the at-home viewer) watch a live-action Western, which leads the Babies to create a Western of their own in their nursery. Their re-enactment/imitation uses elements from a variety of TV programs—a talking horse ("Mr. Ed"), a desert landscape and chases featuring one muppet, Animal, as the "Road Crawler" (from "Looney Tunes") and the "Dallas"-inspired Miss Piggy Sue Ewing, a "modern cowgirl with beauty, brains and a great head for business...just like on nighttime TV."

This intertextuality, Kinder claims, shows children that images and narrative elements can be combined and recombined to fit their creative needs. The meaning attached to any particular image or narrative is "slippery," and children are encouraged to fashion new meanings out of existing symbols. She proposes that the toy tie-ins that accompany most animated children's programs also are helpful in fostering creativity and understanding of narratives. When children reenact familiar plots or create new adventures for their toy characters, she says, they are practicing story creation. While critics argue that these toys foster play that is imitative but not creative, Kinder responds that imitation and recombination of existing forms—what Frederic Jameson calls "pastiche"—is a dominant creative form in today's postmodern society. So, says Kinder, children's programs offer kids not only creative storytelling, but teach viewers that they can take the narrative and make it their own in play.

This intertextuality, of course, is not new in children's programs. "Sesame Street" has been parodying other entertainment experiences for 20 years. It is also not all in the service of empowering creative children. Kinder makes a compelling argument that the interactive nature of TV programs readies children for the world of video games, and that the intertextuality between these forms (and movies as well) is designed to encourage children to see themselves as "gendered commodities around which a whole commercial nexus is organized...and the child comes to believe that this nexus is activated and extended whenever he or she consumes a product." Using the "Teenage Mutant Ninja Turtles" as an illustration, Kinder describes the development of a "supersystem of transmedia intertextuality" in which these characters were featured in comic books, a television series, two feature films and consumer products from more than 55 licensed manufacturers. The supersystem was enormously popular and easily accessible to young audiences, she notes: "American youngsters of all ages, classes and economic backgrounds were able to participate in the system to varying degrees, for almost everyone could afford a quarter to play the arcade game...or slightly more to buy the comic book or the cookies, and practically no one was too young to wear the T-shirt." It also featured two themes that Kinder claims are prevalent in all children's entertainment: 1) male dominance (the Turtles and their master are all male), and 2) consumption is power (Turtles consume pizza to enhance their martial arts powers).

These themes and their effects on children's attitudes and behaviors are part of a larger concern about the influence of TV's content. Three of the most problematic content areas are sex and race role representations, sexual and violent behaviors, and advertising.

U.S. television has been widely recognized as a potent socializer of children. Along with the family and formal institutions like church and school, TV provides children with information about society and their role in it. Commercial television programming has been frequently criticized for its representation (or lack) of women and people of color. The criticism reflects concern that TV images can foster the development of negative attitudes about people from underrepresented groups. This is the focus of Gordon L. Berry and Joy Keiko Asamen's *Children and Television* and a guiding theme of Huston's *Big World, Small Screen.*

Television, contends Berry, is an expression of culture that becomes for children a "vehicle for securing and shaping their worldview, [which is] composed of the child's attitudes, values and concepts, as well as how the individual thinks, makes decisions, behaves, and defines events." Although the editors and contributing authors are concerned with the role of television as one influence on the development of all children's worldviews, there is special concern for minority children, who tend to spend more time with the tube than do whites, and who are more likely to come from households where TV is more central to their daily lives. What television presents to these children is a world where people of their own ethnic group are absent or underrepresented, low in status and frequent victims.

Berry and Asamen provide carefully detailed, thorough analyses of the portrayals of minorities and other disadvantaged groups (women, the elderly, people with disabilities) in programs and advertisements designed for children and families on commercial broadcast, public broadcast and cable TV. Not surprisingly, nonwhites, females, the disabled and the elderly are absent or underrepresented in every category of content on commercial television. There is a greater degree of diversity on public TV.

Cable provides some diversity. Nickelodeon features some original programming with culturally diverse casts, as well as "Nick News," which features a multiracial cast and occasionally deals with issues like racism and sexism. Spanish-speaking children who have access to one of the three Hispanic-oriented networks available in the United States can see programs produced in Mexico, Brazil, Peru, Venezuela, Puerto Rico and Spain. These programs are "much more reflective of the diverse ethnic compositions of (Latino) societies" and promote values and moral lessons traditionally promoted by Hispanic families.

A chronicling of the lack of diversity on television is not enough to answer the question of effects of these types of images, however. Many studies indicate that media representations can influence both viewer perceptions of others as well as their self-perceptions. Studies that utilize cultivation analysis have shown consistent, though usually quite small, positive correlations between the amount of television viewed and perceptions that the real world is much like the one presented on television. It is suggested that viewing substantial amounts of television programming leads the viewer to "cultivate" a perception of the real world that is consistent with the TV world. Heavy TV viewing can lead, two of the authors suggest, to the belief that there are few women or minorities in high-level professional careers, that women and the elderly are frequent victims of crime, or that women are happiest at home raising children.

Essential to the cultivation hypothesis is the belief that all commercial television presents basically the same ideological picture of the world, so that specific viewing patterns are irrelevant: It doesn't matter if one spends 30 hours with network TV or 30 hours with MTV, the same perceptions would be cultivated. And it is here that this theory runs into trouble. Many critics have called for a reformulation of the cultivation hypothesis to account for unique or anomalous programs and characters—the Murphy Browns or the Cliff Huxtables or the Al Bundys. The impact of a highly salient character may be more powerful than that of several "usual" characters.

To account for the influence of individual characters or programs, other analysts have applied social learning theory, which holds that viewers learn through observing the social behavior of models—and television is a prolific source of models. Viewers use television's messages to create cognitive frameworks of the world and to enhance existing frameworks. Using this formulation, it is possible to see how both general patterns of representation as well as unique television characters and programs could influence children's worldviews.

Although the belief that television portrayals can influence attitudes has prompted many interest groups to protest their representation on television, there has been surprisingly little research done on these effects. The few studies described in Comstock and Paik, Huston, and

Berry and Asamen indicate that television portrayals can influence children's perceptions of themselves and others, but the results are often conflicting. For instance, Sherryl Brown Graves (in Berry and Asamen) cites one study that showed that exposure to cartoons featuring African American characters, regardless of the type of portrayal, produced positive racial attitudes in African American subjects. On the other hand, she reports that a different study found that exposure to same-group characters produced negative attitudes in African American children. For white children, the direction of influence (i.e., viewers expressing positive or negative attitudes towards a particular group) is consistent with the type of portrayal presented. For example, after two years of viewing the racially integrated "Sesame Street," white children expressed more positive attitudes toward African Americans and Latinos.

Due probably to the lack of representations of minority groups other than women and African Americans on commercial television, there is almost no research on the effects of other types of representations presented in these volumes. However, the research on the influence of portrayals of women and African Americans leads to two generalizations. First, exclusion and negative portrayals of group members foster both lower levels of self-esteem and more negative attitudes towards members of that group. Second, carefully planned programming can have positive effects on viewers attitudes and self-concepts.

Several chapters in *Media, Children and the Family* provide thorough descriptions of the amount and types of sexual content in American media. As to the effect of these portrayals on the attitudes and sexual behaviors of young users, author James B. Weaver III suggests two models: the sexual communication model, which posits that sexually oriented materials offer instruction and therapy to users; and the sexual callousness model, which posits that these materials foster "detrimental perceptions of female sexuality, a misogynous cultural climate, and promote intergender violence." Most of the evidence presented in *Media, Children and the Family* supports the sexual callousness model. Authors Jennings Bryant and Steven Carl Rockwell suggest that "massive" exposure (three hours/night for five consecutive nights) to prime-time, sexually oriented programming influenced the moral judgment of 13- and 14-year-olds. Specifically, teens who had been exposed to such programming in their experiment rated a series of sexual indiscretions and improprieties as "less bad" and described the victim as "less wronged" than did teens who had not seen the programs; teens from families with clearly defined value systems and an open style of communication, however, were less affected by the content.

The question of advertising targeting children has also been of major concern, particularly in terms of the content of the advertisements and children's abilities to understand the messages. Critics charge that the products advertised to children promote unhealthy lifestyles. Content analyses have consistently shown that the most frequently advertised products during children's programs are food—sugared cereals, candy, snacks and fast food, with toy advertisements rivaling food ads in number during the Christmas season. Studies also have shown that advertisements influence children's desires for products, with heavily advertised products seen as more desirable than unadvertised products. So it's not surprising that heavy TV viewing is related to more child insistence to buy products, an indirect consequence being parent-child conflict. In fact, some studies have found that elementary school children would become aggressive, feel bad and not want to play with their parents when denied their purchase requests, report Comstock and Paik.

Most evidence over the past two decades indicates that preschool children are often unable to distinguish commercials from programs; those who can usually make a perceptual distinction rather than a conceptual one. That is, young children might distinguish ads from programs by their length and the fact that they deal with consumer goods; only in rare instances do they use the persuasive nature of advertisements as a distinguishing factor. This recognition is important, at least theoretically, because it encourages viewers to be skeptical of the content. Researchers have used the term "cognitive defense" to refer to the ability to recognize and understand the nature of persuasion, and studies have shown that these defenses are crucial to allowing children to resist persuasive messages. These defenses are often not displayed in children before the age of 7 or 8, making it an ethical dilemma for policy-makers to allow advertising to audiences who are too young to understand its intent.

But, because advertising revenue is considered essential for the existence of children's programming, policy-makers have been reluctant to ban ads targeting children. In an effort to decrease the amount of children's exposure to ads, the 1990 Children's Television Act prescribes time limits for commercials aired during children's programs. To address the problem of children's inability to distinguish programs from commercials, the television industry voluntarily created program-commercial separators—those five-second messages that announce, "We'll be back after these messages"—as a signal to young children. These have been shown to be mostly ineffective, however: If children do not know what an ad is, then what difference does it make to know that one is coming up?

What other options exist? One is the recognition that some children at young ages are able to both distinguish programs from commercials *and* recognize the selling intent of advertisements. It is an awareness that can be taught. A section on advertising should be included in any media education curriculum created for preschool and early elementary school students.

But even the most carefully crafted advertising educational intervention may fall short of its goal of reducing children's eagerness for advertised products. As Ellen Seiter argues in *Sold Separately,* advertising and children's products are important parts of children's culture in this country. "Children's interest in consumer culture involves much more than greed, hedonism or passivity," she suggests: "It involves the desire for community and for a utopian freedom from adult authority, seriousness and goal-directedness. As a mass culture, toys and television give children a medium of communication."

Seiter analyzes the content of children's product advertisements in parents' magazines and children's television to show that parent-targeted ads tout the ability of products to please and enrich the lives of children. Child-targeted ads, on the other hand, show a world where "kids rule" and fun is the order of the day.

This separateness from the adult world, and celebration of peer culture, is one reason for the high appeal of children's advertisements, products and programs, as Seiter discusses. Boys and girls want to participate in their peer culture, and television provides them with the means to do that. Not only do ads offer information about toys and other goods that are peer-approved and parent-disapproved (or so the ads indicate), but the ads themselves are often a basis for peer interaction. Children swap knowledge of different products, slogans and jingles as a way of achieving solidarity.

In the same way that Kinder suggests that toy-based television programs and their attendant toys empower children creatively, Seiter claims these combinations foster social relationships and the building of peer culture. But, like Kinder, she recognizes the problem inherent in children's culture being created not by children, but by international entertainment conglomerates run by adults whose interests are in creating consumers, not creative playmates. This helps explain why the world of children's television is, according to Seiter, "utopian in some respects.... [Although] access to this child-centered utopia is restricted; full citizenship is denied to girls of all races and to boys of color."

Through her careful analysis of children's television commercials, Seiter finds patterns common to such examination—that girls and children of color are marginalized or excluded from participation in most advertisements. Children's ads, she suggests, "bind children together as an audience defined in opposition to adults—by encouraging a social identity based on age, by ridiculing and inverting the values of adult culture. At the same time, they segment the children's audiences in the same ways that the U.S. film and television industries historically have segmented adults—most importantly and blatantly by gender, more subtly by race and ethnicity." She suggests that to successfully teach children about the ways that commercials work, "they need to be discussed not only in terms of 'selling intent,' but also in terms of the repertoire of visual and aural signs that help to form children's common vocabulary. Any media education program should concern itself not only with the discriminatory but with the utopian aspects of children's commercials as well."

These six new books address concerns regarding children and media, providing evidence that television is a very effective teacher of some information to some children under some conditions. Individual differences in children's mental abilities, interests, motivations for viewing, family orientation to media and cultural backgrounds (to name just a few) all contribute to the variability in use and responses to content. What this variability means for parents and educators is that media use can be a positive experience for any child. The challenge is making it so. What this variability means for media researchers is that, while there is a large and growing literature in this area, we are far from figuring it all out.

Katharine E. Heintz is assistant professor in the School of Communications at the University of Washington.

24

The Guardians of Growing Up— A User's Guide to Children and Media Research Groups

Dirk Smillie

From the mid-1920s to the early 1930s, radio evolved from a techno-logical miracle to a standard American household fixture. Its emerging centrality to the nation's culture was quickly recognized, first by the regulatory framework of the Federal Radio Act of 1927 and then by the Communications Act of 1934. But as Congress and corporate America focused on the power and influence of radio in the adult world, educa-tors, social science researchers and others wondered what impact the new medium would have on children. That was the question taken up in the mid-1930s by a study group in Madison, Wis., formed by members of the American Association of University Women. The group—known today as the National Telemedia Council—met regularly to evaluate radio programs in news, drama and music for both children and adults. As perhaps the oldest children's media literacy organization in the na-tion, it was followed by what has today become a cottage industry of scholars, advocates, media watchdog groups and research institutes across the nation devoted to improving the wide range of media that kids watch, read, play and listen to.

A significant growth curve in organizations focusing on children and the media followed a period in television history in which children's programming became a profit center on network television for the first time. As network programs shifted from program sponsorship to direct advertising in the early 1960s, children's programs suddenly became lucrative. In 1965, children's Saturday-morning programs carried as many as 16 commercial minutes per hour, despite the FCC Television Code's restriction of 9.5 minutes for adult programming.

But what drew the ire of children's television activists wasn't advertising. As author and media critic Les Brown writes, "Citizens' groups did not become aroused...until the networks began to deal excessively—in their competitive zeal—with monsters, grotesque superheroes and gratuitous violence to win the attention of youngsters."

Today, the landscape of groups devoted to children and the media is filled with far more than advocates and activists. Universities are home to institutes and study centers grappling with issues like the cognitive influences of "Barney & Friends" and how kids can connect to the information superhighway. Academe, often in partnership with foundations, is helping in other ways, such as the University of Maryland's new Casey Journalism Center for Children and Families, Harvard's Institute on Media Education, and the Prudential Foundation-funded fellows program at the Columbia Graduate School of Journalism to help journalists hone their reporting skills on the children's beat.

Organizations focusing on children and the media can be found throughout the United States, from northern California to the Rust Belt, from the Midwest to Washington. While many are research-driven, funded by government and foundation grants, others are decidedly political, serving as advocates and watchdogs that lobby Congress and the Federal Communications Commission. Although agenda vary greatly from one group to another, it's of little surprise that the influence of television is overwhelmingly the primary focus.

And perhaps for good reason. The average 2- to 11-year-old spends nearly 22 hours per week watching broadcast and cable television, notes the 1994 edition of *TV Dimensions,* an annual report on television audience, advertising and revenue trends. Weekly use of video games and home videos adds an average of another three hours, bringing the time kids spend in front of the television to about 25 hours a week. That time is the focus of the half-dozen organizations devoted to media literacy for children formed in the early 1990s alone.

What follows is a listing of some of the major organizations dedicated to the study, research and advocacy of issues related to children and the media. This list does not include producers of children's media—Children's Express, Youth Communication, Lucky Duck Productions, Children's Television Workshop, KidNews and Nickelodeon, to name but a few—even though many such organizations are involved in varying degrees with children's media literacy, research or education. Instead, our aim is to provide an overview of the institutions whose primary focus is research and study of children and media—their interests, issues and resources—along with information on how to contact them.

Casey Journalism Center for Children and Families
University of Maryland
College Park, Md. 20742-7111
(301) 405-2482

Director: Cathy Trost
Founded: 1993
Annual budget: $350,000
Full-time staff: 2
Purpose: To enhance reporting about the issues and institutions affecting disadvantaged children and their families.
Highlights: Annual conference on emerging issues related to children and families.

Center for Children and Technology
Education Development Center
96 Morton Street, 7th Floor
New York, N.Y. 10014
(212) 633-8230

Director: Jan Hawkins
Founded: 1981
Annual budget: $1.5 to $2.5 million
Full-time staff: 25
Purpose: Investigates, through research and development, the key roles technologies can play in affecting education through computer, video and telecommunications as tools for educational change.
Highlights: Will inaugurate "Media Workshop New York" this fall, funded by the Bertelsmann Foundation to help New York City school teachers develop students' media literacy skills.

Center for Media Education
1511 K Street, N.W., Suite 518
Washington, D.C. 20005
(202) 628-2620

Director: Jeffrey Chester
Founded: 1991
Annual budget: $500,000
Full-time staff: 6
Purpose: To improve children's television programming and monitor compliance with the Children's Television Act of 1990 through the Campaign for Kids' TV, a project of the Center started in 1991.
Highlights: The Center's Maryland Campaign for Kids TV has mobilized the involvement of senior citizens, businesses and parents in a collaborative public education effort to improve children's television. The campaign has also produced report cards grading 15 television stations in Maryland and Washington to encourage their compliance with the Children's Television Act.

Center for Media Literacy
1962 S. Shenandoah Street
Los Angeles, Calif. 90034
(310) 559-2944

Executive Director and Founder: Elizabeth Thoman
Founded: 1985
Annual budget: varies between $350,000 to $500,000
Full-time staff: 5
Purpose: To help children and adults prepare for living and learning in a global media culture by translating media literacy research and theory into practical information, training and education tools for teachers and youth leaders, parents and care givers of children.
Highlights: The Center's largest project to date, a media violence kit titled *Beyond Blame: Challenging Violence in the Media,* was released in November 1994. The kit, a learning series for teachers to use with elementary, middle- and high school students, is designed to educate them about the myths and truths of violence in the media.

Center for Research on the Influences of Television on Children (CRITC)
Department of Human Development
4001 Dole Hall
University of Kansas
Lawrence, Kan. 66045-2133
(913) 864-4646

Directors: Aletha C. Huston and John C. Wright
Founded: 1976
Annual budget: $150,000 to $300,000 (variable)
Full-time staff: 4 full time; (plus 12 half-time grad students)
Purpose: To conduct research on ways in which television is processed by children, tracking both positive and negative effects of television on childhood development.
Highlights: CRITC is known for its developmental research on television in the McLuhan tradition.

Children and the Media Project
Children Now
1212 Broadway, Suite 513
Oakland, Calif. 94612
(510) 763-2444

Director: Vicky Rideout
Founded: 1993
Program budget: varies between $200,000 to $400,000
Full-time staff: 2
Purpose: To examine the impact of the media on children, looking both at kids as consumers of media and how children are affected by it.
Highlights: Sponsored first national conference on children and the news media in 1994, keynoted by first lady Hillary Rodham Clinton, which drew attention to the impact of violence in the media on children.

Children's Television Resource and Education Center
340 Townsend Street, Suite 423
San Francisco, Calif. 94107
(415) 243-9943

President: Parker Page
Founded: 1985
Annual budget: $250,000 to $400,000
Full-time staff: 5 (plus 10–12 contractors and consultants)
Purpose: To provide services and products related to children and television for parents and teachers that promote children's social development, creativity and academic achievement.
Highlights: Produced "The Adventures of Christina Valentine," an audiotape series about a teen-ager who looks to television to solve real-life problems, which has won awards from the Corporation for Public Broadcasting and the American Library Association.

Downs Media Education Center
223 N. Guadalupe, No. 259
Santa Fe, N.M. 87501
(505) 820-1129

Director: Deirdre Downs
Founded: 1991
Annual budget: variable
Full-time staff: variable—mainly grass-roots volunteers
Purpose: To create a media-literate culture, training teachers, parents, government and members of the media to effect media literacy among children.
Highlights: The Center's National Media Literacy project is supported by both the Departments of Labor and Education and has played a key role in developing Las Cruces, N.M., as the first media-literate city in the United States.

Institute on Media Education
339 Gutman Library
Harvard Graduate School of Education
Cambridge, Mass. 02138
(617) 239-4975

Director: Renée Hobbs
Founded: 1993
Annual budget: $50,000 to $100,000 (variable per year)
Full-time staff: 3

Purpose: To raise public awareness of how media industries work and to encourage teachers to work with students in better analyzing and understanding media content.
Highlights: Were heavily oversubscribed in registration for the institute in 1994.

Kidsnet
6856 Eastern Ave., N.W.
Washington, D.C. 20012
(202) 291-1400

Founder and Executive Director: Karen Jaffe
Founded: 1984
Annual budget: $300,000
Full-time staff: 4
Purpose: A computerized clearinghouse of audio, video, radio and television programming for young people from preschool age through high school. Also develops curricular material around television programs for dissemination to educators, health and social service professionals.
Highlights: In 1992, Jaffe was appointed to the Council of the National Endowment for Children's Educational Television.

National Telemedia Council
120 East Wilson Street
Madison, Wis. 53703
(608) 257-7712

Executive Director: Marieli Rowe
Founded: 1953
Annual budget: $50,000
Full-time staff: all-volunteer
Purpose: To promote critical television-viewing skills and media literacy for children and to link the efforts of teachers, librarians, media specialists, parents and other care givers in helping children to be in rather than under the control of the media.
Highlights: Has established a clearinghouse and database consisting of several thousand entries on experts, publications and resources on media literacy.

National Video Resources
73 Spring Street, Room 606
New York, N.Y. 10012
(212) 274-8080

Executive Director: Timothy Gunn
Founded: 1990
Budget: $500,000 to $700,000
Full-time staff: 3
Purpose: To assist in the distribution to parents of high-quality, independently produced children's film and video.
Highlights: One of the few groups dedicated to offering independently produced children's programming.

Prudential Fellows Program for Children and the News
Columbia Graduate School of Journalism
Columbia University
New York, N.Y. 10027
(212) 854-3319

Director: David Klatell
Founded: 1994
Annual budget: $350,000
Full-time staff: 3
Purpose: A three-year grant from the Prudential Foundation will allow four journalists annually to attend courses at the Columbia Graduate School of Journalism, participate in special seminars with outside experts and extend their knowledge in a variety of aspects related to covering children's issues, including legal and ethical issues.

Strategies for Media Literacy
1095 Market Street, Suite 617
San Francisco, Calif. 94103
(415) 621-2911

Founder and Director: Kathleen Tyner
Founded: 1986
Annual budget: $25,000 to $50,000 (varies)

Full-time staff: 2
Purpose: To promote media education through weeklong media literacy institutes and on-line dissemination of media education resources.
Highlights: Media & You: An Elementary Media Literacy Curriculum Guide, written for parents and teachers, and *The Critical Eye: Inside TV Advertising,* a resource for secondary students available on interactive videodisc with Hypercard.

The Children's Partnership
1460 Fourth Street, Suite 306
Santa Monica, Calif. 90401
(310) 260-1220

Co-Founders and Co-Directors: Wendy Lazarus and Laurie Lipper
Founded: 1993
Budget: $100,000 to $200,000
Full-time staff: 3 (plus project consultants)
Purpose: To place the needs of America's 67 million children at the forefront of emerging national policy debates via the public and the media and to function as a research and development arm for the children's movement.
Highlights: In September 1994, the Partnership published *America's Children and the Information Superhighway: A Briefing Book and National Action Agenda,* the first comprehensive analysis of how the information superhighway and other new media affect children.

Yale University Family Television Research and Consultation Center
Department of Psychology
Yale University
Box 208205
New Haven, Conn. 06520-8205
(203) 432-4565

Co-Directors: Dorothy G. and Jerome L. Singer
Founded: 1976
Annual budget: variable, based on project
Full-time staff: 4 (hires additional researchers based on project)

Purpose: Conduct research on impact of television on children and youth; provide consultation and evaluation of programming aimed at youth; advise parents, educators and health care specialists on use of media for child and adolescent development.

Highlights: Just published *Creating Critical Viewers,* a television literacy manual for middle- and high school students.

For Further Reading

Action for Children's Television, Kim Hays, ed. *TV, Science & Kids: Teaching Our Kids to Question.* Reading, Mass.: Addison-Wesley, 1984.

Aimiller, Kurt. *Television and Young People: A Bibliography of International Literature.* New York: K.G. Saur, 1989.

America's Children: What Can, What Should, the Media Do to Save the Next Generation? Nieman Reports, Vol. 47, No. 1, Spring 1993.

Barcus, Francis E. *Images of Life on Children's Television: Sex Roles, Minorities and Families.* New York: Praeger, 1983.

———. *Children's Television: An Analysis of Programming and Advertising.* New York: Praeger, 1977.

Barry, Thomas E. *Children's Television Advertising.* Chicago: American Marketing Association, 1977.

Beels, Jessica, ed. *Kids' Voices Count: Illuminating the Statistics.* Washington, D.C.: Children's Express, 1994.

Berry, Gordon L. and Joy Keiko Asamen. *Children and Television: Images in a Changing Sociocultural World.* Newbury Park, Calif.: Sage, 1993.

———. *Television and the Socialization of the Minority Child.* New York: Academic Press, 1982.

Bettelheim, Bruno. *The Uses of Enchantment: The Meaning and Importance of Fairytales.* New York: Vintage Books, 1977.

Boyer, Ernest. *Ready to Learn: A Mandate for the Nation.* Princeton, N.J.: The Carnegie Foundation for the Advancement of Teaching, 1993.

Bryant, Jennings, and Daniel R. Anderson, eds. *Children's Understanding of Television: Research on Attention and Comprehension.* New York: Academic Press, 1983.

Bryant, Jennings, ed. *Television and the American Family.* Hillsdale, N.J.: Erlbaum, 1990.

Cater, Douglass. *TV Violence and the Child.* New York: Russell Sage Foundation, 1975.

Charren, Peggy, and Martin W. Sandler. *Changing Channels: Living (Sensibly) with Television.* Reading, Mass.: Addison-Wesley, 1983.

Chen, Milton. *The Smart Parent's Guide to Kids' TV.* San Francisco: KQED Books, 1994.

Children and Family Journalism: Out from the Shadows. Survey of Media Coverage of Children's Issues by the Casey Journalism Center for Children and Families of the College of Journalism. College Park, Md.: University of Maryland, 1994.

Children and the Media: Proceedings of the First International Conference, Los Angeles 1985. Los Angeles: Children's Institute International/Paris: Centre International de l'Enfance, 1987.

Children's Television Workshop and Educational Testing Service. *Sesame Street Research: A 20th Anniversary Symposium.* New York and Princeton N.J., 1990

Cole, John Y. *Television, the Book, and the Classroom.* Washington: Library of Congress, 1978.

Comstock, George, and Haejung Paik. *Television and the American Child.* San Diego: Academic Press, 1991.

Copperman, Paul. *Taking Books to Heart: How to Develop a Love of Reading in Your Child.* Reading, Mass.: Addison-Wesley, 1986.

Corporation for Public Broadcasting. *Study of School Uses of Television and Video: Summary Report.* Washington, D.C., 1992.

Crane, Valerie, ed. *Informal Science Learning: What Research Says About Television, Science Museums and Community-Based Projects.* Dedham, Mass.: Research Communications, Ltd., 1994.

Dorfman, Ariel. *How to Read Donald Duck: Imperialist Ideology in the Disney Comic.* 2nd ed. Trans. David Kunzle. New York: International General, 1984.

Dorr, Aimee. *Television and Children: A Special Medium for a Special Audience.* Beverly Hills, Calif.: Sage Publications, 1986.

Durkin, Kevin. *Television, Sex Roles, and Children: A Developmental Social Psychological Account.* Philadelphia: Open University Press, 1985.

Eberle, Paul and Shirley Eberle. *The Abuse of Innocence: The McMartin Preschool Trial.* Buffalo, N.Y.: Prometheus Books, 1993.

Emerson, Adrian. *Teaching Media in the Primary School.* New York: Cassell, 1993.

Fischer, Stuart. *Kid's TV: The First 25 Years.* Faction File Publications, 1983.

Focus on Children: The Beat of the Future. Report of the 1992 Media Conference at the Columbia University Graduate School of Journalism, 1992.

Goodwillie, Susan, ed. *Violence in the Child's Life: At Home, At School and On the Streets.* Washington: Children's Express, 1994.

Greenfield, Patricia Marks. *Mind and Media: The Effects of Television, Video Games and Computers.* Cambridge: Harvard University Press, 1984.

Grossman, Gary. *Saturday Morning TV.* New York: Dell, 1981.

Group for the Advancement of Psychiatry. Committee on Social Issues. *The Child and Television Drama: The Psychosocial Impact of Cumulative Viewing.* New York: Mental Health Materials Center, 1982.

Gunter, Barrie. *Children and Television: The One-Eyed Monster?* New York: Routledge, 1990.

Hartley, Ian. *Goodnight Children—Everywhere.* New York: Hippocrene Books, 1983.

Healy, Jane. *Endangered Minds: Why Our Children Don't Think.* New York: Simon & Schuster, 1990.

Hodge, Bob, and David Tripp. *Children and Television: A Semiotic Approach.* Cambridge, U.K.: Polity Press, 1986.

Holland, Patricia. *What is a Child? Popular Images of Childhood.* London: Virago, 1992.

Home, Anna. *Into the Box of Delights: A History of Children's Television.* London: BBC Books, 1993.

Huston, Aletha C. et al. *Big World, Small Screen: The Role of Television in American Society.* Lincoln, Neb.: University of Nebraska Press, 1992.

Huston, Aletha C., and John C. Wright. Effects of Educational TV Viewing of Lower Income Pre-Schoolers on Academic Skills, School Readiness, and School Adjustment One to Three Years Later: A Report to Children's Television Workshop. University of Kansas, 1995.

Kinder, Marsha. *Playing with Power in Movies, Television and Video Games.* Berkeley, Calif.: University of California Press, 1991.

Kline, Stephen. *Out of the Garden: Toys, TV and Children's Culture in the Age of Marketing.* London: Verso, 1993.

Kotlowitz, Alex. *There Are No Children Here: The Story of Two Boys Growing Up in the Other America.* New York: Doubleday, 1991.

Liebert, Robert M. *The Early Window: Effects of Television on Children and Youth.* 3rd ed. New York: Pargamon Press, 1988.

Linkletter, Art. *Kids Say the Darndest Things.* Ottawa, Ill.: Green Hill Publishers, 1957.

Luke, Carmen. *Constructing the Child Viewer: A History of American Discourse on Television and Children, 1950–1980.* New York: Praeger, 1990.

Lull, James, ed. *World Families Watch Television.* Newbury Park: Sage, 1988.

Lurie, Alison. *Don't Tell the Grown-ups: Subversive Children's Literature.* Boston: Little, Brown, 1990.

Lusted, D., ed. *Television and Schooling.* London: BFI/London Institute of Education, 1985.

McNeal, James U. *Children as Consumers: Insights and Implications.* Lexington, Mass.: Lexington Books, 1987.

Messenger, Maire. *Television Is Good for Your Kids.* London: Shipman, 1989.

Moody, Kate. *Growing Up on Television.* New York: McGraw-Hill, 1984.

Morley, D. *Family Television: Cultural Power and Domestic Leisure.* London: Comedia, 1986.

Paley, Vivian Gussin. *Boys & Girls: Superheroes in the Doll Corner.* Chicago: University of Chicago Press, 1984.

Palmer, Edward L. *Television and America's Children: A Crisis of Neglect.* New York: Oxford University Press, 1988.

_____. *Children in the Cradle of Television.* Lexington, Mass.: Lexington Books, 1987.

Palmer, Edward L., and Aimee Dorr, eds. *Children and the Faces of Television: Teaching, Violence, Selling.* New York: Academic Press, 1980.

Postman, Neil. *Amusing Ourselves to Death.* New York: Viking Penguin, 1985.

_____. *The Disappearance of Childhood.* New York: Delacorte Press, 1982.

Provenzo, Eugene F. Jr. *Video Kids: Making Sense of Nintendo.* Cambridge: Harvard University Press, 1991.

Rosengren, Karl E. *Media Matter: TV Use in Childhood and Adolescence.* Norwood, N.J.: Ablex Publishing Corp., 1989.

Rubenstein, Eli A., and Jane D. Brown. *The Media, Social Science, and Social Policy for Children.* Norwood, N.J.: Ablex Publishing Corp., 1985.

Schneider, Cy. *Children Communicating.* Lincolnwood, Ill.: NTC Business Books, 1987.

_____. *Children's Television: The Art, the Business and How It Works.* Lincolnwood, Ill.: NTC Business Books, 1987.

Seiter, Ellen. *Sold Separately: Children and Parents in Consumer Culture.* New Brunswick, N.J.: Rutgers University Press, 1993.

Simpson, P., ed. *Parents Talking Television.* London: Comedia, 1987.

Singer, Jerome L., and Dorothy G. Singer. *Television, Imagination, and Aggression: A Study of Preschoolers.* Hillsdale, N.J.: L. Erlbaum Associates, 1981.

Stern, Sydney Ladensohn, and Ted Schoenhaus. *Toyland: The High-Stakes Game of the Toy Industry.* Chicago: Contemporary Books, 1990.

Sutton-Smith, Brian. *Toys as Culture.* New York: Gardner Press, 1986.

Television Viewing Lab. *Couch Potato Chronicles: Children's Television Viewing.* Boston: WGBH, February 1994.

Turow, Joseph. *Entertainment, Education, and the Hard Sell: Three Decades of Network Children's Television.* New York: Praeger, 1981.

Voort, T. H. A. van der. *Television Violence: A Child's-eye View.* New York: Elsevier Science Pub. Co., 1986.

Ward, Scott, Tom Robertson, and Ray Brown, eds. *Commercial Television and European Children: An International Research Digest.* Brookfield, Vt.: Gower, 1986.

Wartella, Ellen, ed. *Children Communicating: Media and the Development of Thought, Speech, Understanding.* Beverly Hills: Sage, 1979.

White, P., ed. *Pushing Smoke: Tobacco Advertising and Promotion.* Copenhagen: World Health Organization Regional Office for Europe and the Commission of the European Communities, 1988.

Winn, Marie. *Unplugging the Plug-In Drug*. New York: Viking Penguin, 1987.

Winship, Elizabeth C. *Reaching Your Teenager*. New York: Houghton Mifflin, 1983.

Young, Brian M. *Television Advertising and Children*. New York: Oxford University Press, 1990.

Zillman, Dolf, Jennings Bryant and Aletha C. Huston, eds. *Media, Children, and the Family*. Hillsdale, N.J.: Lawrence Erlbaum Associates, 1994.

Index

A&E, 157
ABC, 23, 27, 52, 57, 58, 75, 152–157
"ABC Answering Children's Questions," 156
ABC News, xviii, 49, 114
"ABC World News Tonight," 51
ABC-TV, 123
Academic Press, 161
Accutane, 86
Action for Children's Television, v, xiv, xxi, 16, 19, 22
"Addams Family," 34
"Adventures of Christina Valentine," 180
Aesop, 7
"Aladdin," 153
Alameda Unified School District, 66
Alicia Patterson Foundation, 52
Allen, Francis, xxii
American Agenda, 51, 58
American Association of Retired People, 133
American Association of University Women, 175
American Press Institute, 51
American Psychological Association's Task Force on Television, 163, 164
American University, vi, xxi
America's Children and the information Superhighway: A Briefing, 183
"Amos 'n' Andy," 65
Amusing Ourselves to Death, 83, 114
Anderson, Dr. Daniel, 80
Anne of Green Gables, 82
Annie E. Casey Foundation, 54, 127
Anunkor, Ifeoma, 143, 145, 149
Ariel, 36
Aries, Phillipe, xix
Arizona Republic, 51, 53
Asamen, Joy Keiko, 161, 163, 168, 170
Ask Beth, xxii, 85, 92

Aspen Institute, 104
"Assignment Discovery," 157
AT&T, 146
Atari, 8
Atlanta Constitution, 57
Atlantic Monthly to Parenting, 50
Aufderheide, Patricia, vi, 28
Avonlea, 152, 157

Babson College in Massachusetts, xxii, 111
Baldacci, Leslie, 56
Ball, Dr. Samuel, 80
Barbie and Ken, 44
Barney, xxiii, 35, 45, 52, 75, 82
"Barney & Friends," 78, 176
"Batman," 34
Batten, James, 51
Bazalgette, Cary, 106
"Beakman's World," 23, 24, 26, 78, 152
"Beat of the Future," 54
"Beavis and Butt-Head," 64
Beethoven, xxiii
"Before the Snow Starts," xx, 4
Bell Atlantic, v
Bell Atlantic Video Services, xx, 5
Benzoyl Peroxide, 86
Bergen County, NJ, *Record,* 51, 52
Berry, Gordon L., 161, 163, 168, 170
Bert, 165
Bert and Ernie, viii, xxiii
Bertelsmann Foundation, 177
Best, Rebecca, 149
Betty MacDonald Books, 152
"Beulah," 65
"Beverly Hills 90210," 110
"Beyond Blame: Challenging Violence in the Media," 178
Big Bird, viii, xxiii, 82, 165
Big Wheel, 127

Big World, Small Screen, 161, 163, 164, 168
"Bill Nye the Science Guy," 27, 157
Bly, Nellie, 49
"Bobby's World," 23, 153
Bock, Paula, 132
Bohbot, Allen, 27, 28
"Boy Meets World," 154
Boyer, Ernest, v, xx, 5
"Boyz in the Hood, "137
Bozo, xxiii
Britt, David, 101
Broderbund, 145
Brokaw, Tom, 145
Brown, Jane D., vii, xxii, 72
Brown, Josiah, x, xxiii, 143, 149
Brown, Les, xiv, 176
Brown, Murphy, 169
Bryant, Jennings, 161, 163, 170
Buckingham, David, 106
"Bump in the Night," 155
Bundy, Al, 169
Burch, Dean, 14
Burger, Warren, 19
Burke, James, 82
Burns, Ken, 82
Bush, George, 6
Bush Center in Child Development and Social Policy, 122
"Buy Me That," 156

Cahn, Alice, 155, 156, 157
Campbell, Helen, 49
Campaign for Kids' TV, 178
"Captain Kangaroo," xxiii, 16, 26
Carnegie Foundation, v, xx, 5
Carter, Jimmy, 130
Cartoon Network, 151
Casey, Annie E., 54, 127
Casey Center, 50, 53
Casey Journalism Center, vi, xiv, xxi, 48, 52, 54, 56, 127, 176, 177
Cassidy, Hopalong, 65
CBS, 16, 24, 49, 57, 152, 153, 156
"CBS Schoolbreak," 154
Center for Children and Technology, 177
Center for Education and Lifelong Learning, viii, xxii, 84
Center for Media Education, xxi, 22, 28, 178

Center for Media Literacy, 178
Center for Public Representation, 22
Center for Research on the Influences of Television on Children, 99, 165, 179
Center Stage, 157
Center's National Media Literacy, 180
Charren, Peggy, v, xiv, xxi, 13, 19, 22
Chase, Rebecca, 50, 52
Chen, Iris, xiv
Chen, Milton, viii, xxii, 77, 84
Chester, Jeffrey, 178
Chicago Sun-Times, 51, 53, 56, 138
Chicago Tribune, 47, 51–54, 56, 57, 58, 126, 135
Child, 50
Child Magazine, 162
Children and Television, 161, 163, 168
Children and the Media, xiii, xx, xxi, xxiii, 3, 41, 179
"Children First," 47, 51, 126
"Children Making Television in Guatemala," xviii
Children Now, 55, 56, 62, 179
"Children of the Shadows," 54
Children's Defense Fund New Your Child Health Project, xiv
Children's Express, ix, xiv, xxii, 125–134, 176
Children's Express Journalism Award, 126
Children's Film Festival, 16
Children's Foundation, xviii
Children's Partnership, 183
Children's Television Act, x, xxi, 17, 28, 42, 171, 152, 178
Children's Television Resource and Education Center, 179
Children's Television Workshop, viii, xxi, xxii, 14, 26, 42, 80, 101, 151, 177
Christian Science Monitor, 53
Christian Youth Ministry, 87
Cincinnati Enquirer, 51
Cinderella, 66
"Cisco Kid," 65
City University of New York, 118
Civil War, 82
Clampitt, Robert, ix, xiv, xxii, 125, 134
Clarissa, 155

"Clarissa Explains It All," 154
Clark, Joe, 11
Claster, John, 151
Clinton, Bill, xxiii, 22, 53, 144, 147
Clinton, Hillary Rodham, 53, 179
Close, Sandy, 55
CNN Newsroom, 157
Coffey, Marjani, x, xxiii, 141, 142
College of Communication at the University of Texas-Austin, vi, 37
College of Communication, xxi
Cologne Conference in Germany, 37
Columbia Teachers College in New York, xiv
Columbia University, vi, xiv
Columbia University Graduate School of Journalism, xxi, 45, 54, 127, 176, 182
Commission's Children's Television Unit, 14
Communications Act of 1934, 175
Community Education Services, 96, 97
Computer School News, 145, 147-149
Comstock, George, 161, 163, 164, 169
Comstock and Paik, 171
Conley, Sunny, 116
Connections, 82
Consumer Reports, 156
Cooney, Joan Ganz, 81
"Cops," 109
Coro Foundation, xiv
Council of the National Endowment for Children's Educational Tv, 181
Creating Critical Viewers, 184
Critical Eye: Inside TV Advertising, 183
"Cro," 23, 26, 27, 153, 154, 157
Cronkite, Walter, 130
Cruz, Nephtali, 144
CTW, 81, 95-99, 101
Cunningham, Randall, 25

Dahl, Christopher, ix, xxii, 123
Daily News, 124
Daily Tribune, 55
Daley, Mayor Richard, 130, 136
"Dallas," 166
Dangerfield, Rodney, vi, 47
Daugherty, Jane, 47
Davis, Evelyn, 101
Daw, Nathaniel, xiv

DDAVP, 86
DeLisle, Lisa, xiv
Democratic National Convention, 129
Dennis, Everette E., iii, iv, xv, 126
Denver Post, 49
Department of Education, 10
Department of Human Development, 179
Department of Labor & Education, 180
Department of Psychology, 183
Descriptive Video Service, 152
Des Moines Register, 51
Detroit Free Press, 47, 48, 51, 53, 126
Diary of a Young Girl, 137
DIC Enterprises, 151
Diori, Hamidou, 146
Discovery Channel, 157
Disney, 8, 28, 66, 152, 157
Disney Channel, 152, 157
Dorgan, Byron, 9
"Doug," 152, 155
Doussard, Robin, 128
Downs, Deirdre, 114, 115, 117, 118, 180
Downs, Hugh, 114
Downs Media Education Center, 114, 180
Dutton, E. P., 82
Duvall, Shelley, 152

Eastside Parent, 162
"Edith Ann," 155
Education Development Center, 177
Eggo Mini Waffles, 104
Eisenberg, Jana, v, vi, vii, ix, xx, 3, 8, 41, 69, 121
Electronic Childhood, xxi
Electronic Media, 151
Ellerbee, Linda, vi, xxi, 42, 71, 157
Engel, Margaret, 52, 53
Ernie, 165
Ernie Pyle Award, 54
Escalante, Jaime, 11
"ET," 8

Family Channel, 152, 157
"Family Double Dare," 154
"Family Matters," 75
Federal Communications Commission, v, xx, 12, 13, 22, 145, 146, 152, 176
Federal Radio Act of 1927, 175

"Feed Your Mind," 157
Fellowship Program for Children and the
    News, xxi, 45
Ferris, Charles, 15
Ferris, Linda, xviii
FidoNet's K12Net, 146
First Amendment, The, xiii
Fite, Dr. Katharine, 79
Flintstones, 34
Flowers for Algernon, 104
"Focus on Children," 54
Ford, Gerald, 14
Fowler, Mark, 16, 24
Fox, 34, 75, 153, 154, 156
Fox Children's Network, 155
France, Howard, 24-26
Francis, Allen, ix, 124
Frank, Anne, 137-139
Fred Flintstone, xxiii
Free Education Mail, 146
"Free Willy," 153, 154
Freedman, Samuel, vi, xxi, 45
Freedom Forum Media Studies Center,
    vii, xiv, x, xi, xv,xxi-xxiii, 37, 149
"From Unseen to Unheard to Kidsbeat,"
    xxi
"Full House," 75, 154

"G.I. Joe," 14, 17, 21, 22
Gannett News Service, 126
Garton, Jane Dwyre, 131, 132
Georgetown University, 22
"Ghostbusters," 34
"Ghostwriter," 78, 82, 151, 156
Giles, Gilbert, 130
Gitlin, Todd, vii, xxii, 70
Global Lab, 146
GOALS 2000, 97, 98
Goettsch, Scherrie, 55
Gonzales, Consuelo, 116
"Good things come in small packages,"
    23
Goodrich, Lawrence, 53
Gorelick, Steven, xiv
Graduate School of the City University
    of New York, xiv
Graves, Sherryl Brown, 170
Greeley, Horace, xxiii
Green, Pamela, 101
Greenfield, Patricia, 36

Grover, xxiii
Growing Up on Television, 118
"Guardians of Growing Up," xxi
"Gulliver's Travels," 28
Gunn, Timothy, 182
Gutierrez, Maria Elena, vii, xxii, 63, 66
Guttenplan, Don, xiv

Hamidou, 149
Hart, Erin, ix, xxii, 121
Hart, Julia, ix, xxii, 121
Harvard, vi, xiv, xxi, xxii, 42
Harvard Graduate School of Education,
    19, 180
Harvard Institute on Media Education,
    viii, 111, 176
"Harvest of Shame," 49
Hawkins, Jan, 177
HBO, 152, 156
"He-Man," 23, 75
Healing and the Mind, 82
Healy, Dr. Jane, 78
Heintz, Katherine, x, xxiii, 161, 173
Hermosa Heights Elementary School,
    116
Hernandez, Jose, 149
Herr, Susan, ix, xxiii, 55, 135, 139
"Hey Dude," 154
Heward, Andy, 151
"Hi, Renso," 143
Hobbs, Renee, viii, xxii, 103, 111, 180
Hollestelle, Kay, xviii
Hollings, Ernest, 9
"Home Improvement," 75
Horner, Vivian, v, xx, 5
Horowitz, Irving Louis, xv
House Committee on Children, Youth
    and Families, 71
Houston Chronicle, 57
Hundt, Reed, v, xx, 9, 12, 148
Hunter College, ix, xxii, 118
Hustad, Kathleen, 127
Huston, Aletha C., 99, 161, 163-166,
    168, 169, 179
Huxtable, Cliff, 169
Hypercard, 183

"In the News," 16
In These Times, 28
Indianapolis Star, 126

Indiana University, 131
Inouye, Daniel, 9
Institute on Media Education, xxii, 180
Instructor Magazine, 162

Jackson, Michael, 34, 59
Jaffe, Karen, x, xiv, xxiii, 151, 158, 181
Jameson, Frederic, 167
Jennings, Peter, 156
"Jetsons, The," 17, 22
John D. and Catherine T. MacArthur
    Foundation, 99
Journalism Quarterly, xviii

Kahn, Lori, 154, 155
Kayden, Mimi, 82
KCNC-TV, 27
Kelley, Jennifer, xiv
Kennedy, Robert F., 47, 54
Kentucky Post, 126
"Kid Witness News," 144
KidNews, 177
"Kids Making Media," 121
KIDSNET, x, xiv, xxiii, 158, 181
"Killing Our Children," 51, 54, 55, 135,
    136
Kinder, Marsha, 34, 36, 161, 163, 166,
    167, 172, 173
King, Gov. Bruce, 113, 115
Klatell, David, 182
Knight-Ridder Inc., 51
Kotlowitz, Alex, vi, xxi, 41, 50
KQED, viii, xxii
KQED-TV, 84
Kreck, Carol, 49
Kroeger, Brooke, 49
Kunkel, Dale, vii, xxii, 57, 62

L.A. *Youth,* 138, 142
Lamb Chop, xx, xxiii, 7
"Lamb Chop's Play-Along," 75, 77, 78
Las Cruces Media Literacy Steering
    Committee, 116
Lawrence Erlbaum Associates, 161
Lawson, Carol, 49
Lazarus, Windy, 183
"Lean on Me," 11
Learning Channel, 152
Learning Network, 146
"Leave It to Beaver," 17, 22, 65

Ledger-Star, 51
Leonard, George, 83
Lesser, Gerald, vi, xiv, xxi, 42, 101
Lewis, Shari, v, xx, xxiii, 7, 78, 156
    "Lifestories," 156
Linkletter, Art, v, xx, 7
Linter, Adam, vi, xxi, 43
"Lion King, The," 8
Lipinski, Ann Marie, 52, 56
Lipper, Laurie, 183
"Little Mermaid, The," 36,153
"Long Ago & Far Away," 18
"Loony Tunes," 166
Lopez, Evelyn, 149
Lopez, Kenneth, 147
Los Angeles Times, 57, 58, 138
Lovelace, Valeria, 101
Lucky Duck Productions, xxi, 42, 71,
    176, 177
Lusted, David, 106

MacArthur, Catherine T., 99
MacArthur, John D., 99
MacDonald, Betty, 152
Madison Square Garden, 129
Madonna, 34
"Magic Schoolbus," 151
Magna Carta, 14
Margolies, Lee Heh, 130
Markey, Rep. Edward, 9
Markham, Edwin, 49
Marymount Manhattan College, ix,
    124
Masterman, Len, 106
"Masters of the Maze," 152
McGill, Larry, vii, xxii, 73, 76
McLuhan, 179
*Media & You: An Elementary Media
    Literacy Curriculum Guide,* 183
Media Literacy Day, 113, 117
Media Studies Journal, xiv, xviii
Media Workshop New York, 177
Media, Children and the Family, 161,
    163, 170
Mediascope, 33
Meiklejohn, A., 15
Meriwether, Heath J., 48, 51
Mickey Mouse Club, 23
Microsoft, 151
Mielke, Keith W., viii, xxii, 81, 93, 101

"Mighty Morphin Power Rangers," 21, 25, 28, 64, 75, 79, 153
Mind and Media, 36
Minow, Newton, vi, 6, 21
Miranda, Carmen, 65
Miss Piggy Sue Ewing, 166
"Momma Said," 141
"Monster Force," 153
Moody, Kate, ix, xxii, 118
Morgan, Alan, 115
Morning Journal, 126
"Mortal Kombat," 145
Moyers, Bill, 82, 130
"Mr. Bumpy," 155
"Mr. Ed," 166
Mr. Moose, xxiii
Mr. Rogers, 3
"Mr. Rogers' Neighborhood," vii, 18, 69
"Mr. Wizard," 26
"Mrs. Piggle-Wiggle," 152
Ms., 162
MTV, 157, 169
Mudd, Roger, 130
"Muppet Babies," 166
"Muppet Matinee," 154
Muppets, 34, 80
Murrow, Edward R., 49
"My Little Pony," xxiii, 23, 24, 75
"My Summer as a Girl," 154

"Name Your Adventure," 23
National Association of Broadcasters, 17
National Cable Television Association, 33
National Center for Educational Statistics, 99
National Conference on Children, 54
National Endowment for Children's Educational Television, 32
National Geographic Kids Network, 146
National Information Infrastructure, 144
National Institute for Mental Health, 163
National Media Literacy Project, 114
National Nielsen, 98
National Ready to Learn Act, 32
National School Network Testbed, 146
National School Safety Center, 88
National Science Foundation, 146, 153, 157
National Telecommunications and Information Administration, 145

National Telemedia Council, 175, 181
National Video Resources, 182
NBC, 23, 57, 76, 153
Neff, Craig, vii, xxii, 71
Neuroscience and Behavior Program, 79
New Expression, x, xxiii, 136-139, 141, 142
New Mexico State University, 116
New Moon—The Magazine for Girls and Their Dreams, 121
New School for Social Research, 149
New York City School, 177
New York Daily News, xiv, 138
New York Evening Journal, 49
New York Newsday, 8, 122, 138
New York Post, 124
New York Society for the Prevention of Cruelty to Animals, 49
New York Society for the Prevention of Cruelty to Children, 49
New York Times, xviii, 49, 51, 54, 55, 57
New York Tribune, 49
New York World, 48, 49
New Yorker, 50, 69
New Youth Connection, 124, 138, 142
Newman, Edwin, 130
News & Observer, 128
"News for Kids," 27
News Media of Stanford University, 54
Newsday, ix, xxii, 50, 122
"Nick News," vi, xxi, 42, 154, 157, 168
Nickelodeon, xxi, 5, 17, 32, 42, 71, 73, 152, 154, 155, 157, 168, 177
Nielsen, 73, 100
Nike, 151
1974 Children's Television Report & Policy Statement, 14, 15
1989 Convention on the Rights of the Child, 15
1990 Children's Television Act, x, xxi, 17, 28, 42, 152, 171, 178
"Ninja Turtles," 14, 17
Nixon, Richard, 14
"Not Just News," 156
"Nova," 83
Nye, Bill, 27, 157

Olympics, 24
Onate High School, 117

Oscar, viii, xxiii
"Ozzie and Harriet," 65
O'Hare, Bucky, 15
O'Neal, Lauren, 135

Pacific News Service, 55
Page, Parker, 180
Paik, Haejung, 161, 163, 164, 169
"Paleoworld," 152
Palmer, Edward, 5
Pancho, 65
Parents Guide to Risky Times and Human Sexuality, 92
Parents Magazine, 50
Parker, Everett C., 12
Patterson, Alicia, 52
Patterson, Gene, 88
Payne Fund Studies, 163
PBS, xxii, 23, 75, 82, 97, 151, 155–157
Pease, Edward C., xiv
Philadelphia Daily News, 51
Philadelphia Inquirer, 47, 51, 54
"Planet of the Apes," 108
Plato, xvii, xix
Playing with Power, 161, 163, 166
Popeye, xxiii
Portland Oregonian, 51
Postman, Neil, 83, 114
"Power of Kids," 151
Preschool Educational Program, 97
Presley, Elvis, 34
Price, Judy, 153
"Prime Time Live," 123
Prudential Fellows Program for Children and the News, 182
Prudential Foundation, 127, 176, 182
Public Broadcasting and the American Library Association, 180
Public Broadcasting Service, xxi, 8, 97
Pulitzer, Joseph, 48
Pulitzer Prize, 135
Pyle, Ernie, 54

Quaker Oats, 19

Radio AAHS, ix
Radio AAHS/Children's Broadcasting Corporation, 123
Raffi, xxi, 44
Ralph Bunche Mini-School, 146–148

Ralph Bunche School for Science and Technology, x, 143–145, 148
Rangel, Charles, 148
Raspberry, William, 50, 54
Rather, Dan, 130
"Reading Rainbow," 78, 81, 82
"Ready to Learn," 97
Reagan, Nancy, 131
Reagan, Ronald, 16, 17, 24, 131
"The Real McCoys,"65
"Real News for Kids," 157
"Reboot," 152
Redmond, Tatiana, 135
Reese, Paul, 143, 146, 147, 149
Reno, Janet, 53
Renso, Vasquez, 143, 146, 148, 149
Retin-A, 86
Ricardo, Ricky, 65
Rideout, Vicky, 179
Riis, Jacob, 49
Riley, Richard, v, xx, 4, 146, 147
"Rimba's Island," 153
Ringo Starr, xxiii
Ritt, Glenn, 52
"Road Crawler," 166
Robert F. Kennedy Journalism Award, 54
Robert Taylor Home, 136
Roberts, Linda, 146–148
Rockwell, Steven Carl, 170
"Rocky and Bullwinkle," xxiii
Rogers, Fred, vii, xxii, 69, 156
"Romper Room," xxiii, 24
"Roundhouse," 152
Rowe, Marieli, 181
"Rugrats," 154, 155
Rushnell, Squire, 27
Rutgers University Press, 161

Sadoff, Michal, 126
Sage, 161
Saige, Ellen, 116
San Jose Mercury News, 51
Santa Fe High School, 116
Saturday Evening Post, 131
"Saturday Night Live," 107
"Saving Arizona's Children," 53
School of Communications at the University of Washington, 28, 173
"Schoolhouse Rock," 26, 27, 154

Schroeder, Patricia, vii, xxii, 71
"Scramble," 24
"Scratch," 27
Seattle Times, 132
Sega, 27
Seiter, Ellen, 161, 163, 172. 173
Senate Commerce Committee, 146
"Sense About Sex," 88
Sergeant Garcia, 65
"Service to Children's Television Idea
    Book," 17
"Sesame Street," viii, xix, xxii, xxiii, 17,
    18, 26, 31, 32, 34, 64, 78-83,
    93-100, 156, 165, 167, 170
Sesame Street Magazine, 82
Sesame Street Parent's Guide, 82
"Shadows," 55
Shining Time Station, 75
Shirk, Martha, 49
Showtime, 155, 157
Silha, Stephen, ix, xxii, 125, 134
Simon, Paul, v, xx, 6, 9
Simpson, Carole, 49, 50
"Simpsons," 34
Singer, Dorothy G., 183
Singer, Jerome, 183
Singleton, John, 137
Sky King, xxiii
Smart Parent's Guide to Kid' TV, 84
Smillie, Dirk, xi, 175
Smurf, 24
"Smurfs," 17, 34, 153
Snadifer, Robert, 41
Snow White, 66
"Society and Change," 50
Society Review, 162
Sold Separately, 161, 163, 172
"Sonic the Hedgehog," 27
Spargo, John, 49
"Special Edition," 157
Special Olympics, 87
Spielberg, 8
Sports Illustrated for Kids, vii, xxii, 71
St. Ignatius College Prep, xxiii, 142
St. Louis Post-Dispatch, 49
St. Petersburg (Fla.) *Times,* 88
"Stand and Deliver," 11
"Star Trek," 100
"Star Wars," 34, 127
Steingard, Beth, 158

"Step by Step," 75
Stevenson, Robert Louis, xvii
Stipp, Horst, 31, 76
Strategies for Media Literacy, 182
"Strawberry Shortcake," 23
"Student Briefing," 122, 138
Stuyvesant, Bedford, 98
Sun-Sentinel, 128
Super Goop, 116
"Super Mario Brothers," 17
"Superhuman Samurai Syber Squad,"
    153
"Superman," 17
Sykes, Dennis, ix, xxiii, 135, 139

Takano, Kent, 27
"Take Your Daughter to Work Day," 138,
    147
Taylor, Paul, 47
Taylor, Robert, 136
TBS, 157
"Teenage Mutant Hero Turtles," 33
"Teenage Mutant Ninja Turtles," 32-36,
    75, 79, 167
Television and America's Children, 5
Television and the American Child, 161,
    163, 164
Television Decoder Circuitry Act of
    1990, 152
Tennessean, The, 126
"Tennessee's Shame: The Forgotten
    Children," 126
There Are No Children Here, 50
"30 Minutes," 16
Thoman, Elizabeth, 178
"3-2-1 Contact," 18
Time, 17, 162
Times, 124
Tomlin, Lily, 155
Tomorrow's Morning, xxi, 43
"Transformers," 23,24
Trentlyn, Jessica, 130
Trias, Jenny, 154, 155
Tribune, 55, 136, 137
Trost, Cathy, vi, xiv, xxi, 47, 56, 177
Truglio, Rosemarie, xiv
Turner Program Services, 157
TV Dimensions, 176
TV Guide, 162
Tyner, Kathleen, 182